BOOKS BY HOWARD MUMFORD JONES

Violence and Reason
The Literature of Virginia in the 17th Century
Belief and Disbelief in American Literature
Jeffersonianism and the American Novel
O Strange New World
History and the Contemporary
Reflections on Learning
American Humanism
The Frontier in American Fiction
The Pursuit of Happiness
The Bright Medusa
The Theory of American Literature
Education and World Tragedy
Ideas in America
The Harp That Once
America and French Culture (1750–1848)

VIOLENCE AND REASON

HOWARD MUMFORD JONES

VIOLENCE AND REASON

A BOOK OF ESSAYS

ATHENEUM *NEW YORK*

1969

FOR

Jack and Emma Dawson

ACKNOWLEDGMENTS

The essays and addresses published here have all been printed elsewhere in whole or in large part, as is made clear on the first page of each. For courteous agreement to the publication of these pieces in this volume, I wish to thank the following:

Middlebury College for "Violence and the Humanist"

The Graduate Journal (University of Texas) for "The Arts in a World of Science"

Harvard Alumni Bulletin for "A Farewell to the English Department," "Campus: Echo or Criticism?" and "The Scholar as American"

The University of Pennsylvania Press for "Scholarship and the Future Tense"

Harvard Educational Review for "The Uses of the Past"

Northern California Foreign Language Newsletter for "Peoples, and Nations, and Tongues"

The University of Utah for "The Once and Future Student"

American Council of Learned Societies for "The Bible from a Literary Point of View"

Journal of the History of Ideas for "The Nature of Literary History"

Massachusetts Historical Society for "Massachusetts, There She Is"

Joseph Blumenthal and The Spiral Press for "The Shrine of the Word"

I have kept the original texts of these essays and addresses, altering them only where time has radically altered a fact or in order to remove blemishes of style. Some repetition remains.

February 1969   HOWARD MUMFORD JONES

CONTENTS

VIOLENCE AND REASON

CREDO

IN SEARCHING out a title for this collection of essays and addresses from the latest two decades of my work as a teacher and citizen, I have sometimes been grimly tempted to call it *Against the Grain,* or if not that, then, after Walter Savage Landor, *The Last Fruit Off an Old Tree.* No one can be more conscious than I am that the doctrine of scholarship and humanistic values explicit or implicit in these pages is not that of the younger generation, the newer academics, or the present tense. It is not that I feel I have lived too late into a world too young, and I do not believe the struggle naught availeth, the labor and the wounds are vain. But I cannot grant that scholarship, one of the oldest and noblest of man's creations, should be swallowed up by self-expression or that the thin, wavering line of contemporary fashion is a better criterion of value than the humane tradition, or that Freud, Jung, and their disciples, though they are later in time, are therefore wiser interpreters of human beings than were Plutarch, Shakespeare, Rembrandt, and Beethoven. I cannot be persuaded that God, who is, I am informed, dead, or the course of history, which, I am given to understand, has no course at all, has miracu-

3

lously endowed a group of young persons under thirty with a grasp on reality denied to everyone, living or dead, who does not or did not belong to so singularly gifted a "generation." I put "generation" in quotation marks because, as I shall presently say, it seems to me a fraudulent classification.

I am called upon to admire the idealism of the young, and in the abstract I do, and sometimes in the concrete as well. If all the young were idealists, the problem would look simpler. Obviously a considerable fraction of the rebellious are mainly bent on mischief. But an untaught idealism, an idealism unwilling to be at once humble and sublime, an idealism lacking in the practical sense of a Jefferson or a Lincoln, seems to me narcissistic and comical. Rebelliousness that drains meaning out of language by reducing it to a small, arcane vocabulary and a plethora of obscenities does not seem to me the noblest birth of time; a doctrine of confrontation that begins by denying the simplest premise of rational discussion, and a philosophy of equality that, were it put into effect, would subject the rest of mankind to the confused, tumultuous emotions of persons barely out of their teens, if that, arouse in me only distaste. Against this crude arrogance humanism from the days of Socrates to the days of Whitehead and beyond has always set its face. Are Marshall McLuhan, Kahlil Gibran, and Professor Marcuse really up to rational discourse? I am unshaken in my belief that individual intelligence is preferable to crowd conformity—is anything more monotonous than the costumes, the habits, and the war-cries of the non-conformists? I think I can be more comfortable with decorum than with dirtiness or the affectation of dirtiness, and I am certain we shall get farther with civilized discussions of complex problems than by name-calling (for example,

4

"fascist pigs," "non-negotiable demands," "doing your thing"), senseless destruction of other people's property, and juvescent nihilism.

Am I, then, opposed to giving Black Americans that place in the sun that has been too long denied them? I am not. When I remember that only a century ago the overwhelming majority of Black Americans could neither read nor write, and then contemplate the amazing progress of this race in the last hundred years, I am lost in admiration. Extraordinary as that progress has been, however, and unjust as the Whites have been, the Blacks are at the moment, inevitably, unable to produce in sufficient numbers persons of that wide range of skills, culture, information, patience, and training, the possession of which has enabled the Whites to staff our colleges and universities so admirably that the United States is now in the forefront of the world in technology, science, medicine, and humane learning. I think the Blacks have been patient too long, but I do not see that impatience will miraculously produce this kind of human being in quantities, and I think the radical among them injure the cause of this people when they assume that looting, shooting, burning, rioting, and a reign of terror are going to impress the Whites with the potentiality for wisdom and patience in this minority group. We have a good many other minority groups, and I can imagine no case in which the Blacks or any other of them are going to take the kingdom of learning by violence. Moreover, I think it important to distinguish propaganda in the classroom (the apparent aim of most of the current demand for "African studies") from that patient, careful, and necessary research that will reveal the strength and splendor no less than the weakness of African culture and of the African contribution to American culture.

5

Don't I think we should do something about poverty, and clear up, clear out, or obliterate the slums? Of course I do. I should also like to abolish or clear up or improve the pollution of our remaining natural resources, our obsolete school buildings, muggings in the public parks, our insane transportation patterns, lung cancer, death on the highways, and the queer assumption of the last few years that the colleges and universities, not Congress, somehow are responsible for the Vietnam war and a variety of other public policies or disasters. But there is an ancient adage to the effect that the poor ye have always with you. Biological and technological misfits have appeared in virtually every culture I know anything about, except possibly the Incan or those hard-boiled races who killed their old women, exposed unwanted or unfit children to be eaten by wild animals, or, when they did not worship idiots, put them to death as clogs on the affairs of the tribe. This is obviously no way to behave. But to assume that because you are poor you are therefore a frustrated man of virtue seems to be also fallacious. Moreover, I should be happier about the idealism of youth for better municipal housekeeping if I had not seen public parks and public streets after a parade of protest or a congress of hippies, and not entered sleazy dormitory rooms, apartment houses rented by young couples, motel or hotel bedrooms just vacated after a party of collegians, or had not to use books so mutilated by the vandalism of young readers as to be a sheer horror. I speak of course only of a fraction of this group, but I think it illuminating that if, after "liberating" a university building, the liberators leave it not only undamaged but clean, this is so rare as to call for special comment by the newspapers. I know of scores of young people who go to work quietly in the slums or in the schools or in the Peace Corps or among retarded children, and I cannot overpraise them.

6

But they are not those who are making all the noise and turning academic presidencies into one of our more dangerous professions.

Don't I believe in equality? In rights? If I didn't, I wouldn't teach. I believe in rights as Jefferson believed in rights, and I believe in equality of opportunity, particularly in education, as did he. He held that mature men should be freed from unreasonable restraint, or tyranny. The Declaration of Independence, however, is written with a decent respect for the opinions of mankind, and I am certain Jefferson could not conceive of rights without responsibilities, something the American Civil Liberties Union is going to have to discover one of these days. If Jefferson was in some sense the theorist of public education in this republic, his doctrine was not populist but aristocratic. He wanted to substitute an aristocracy of talent for an aristocracy of birth. The broad base of elementary education was to insure general literacy among citizens so that they could be informed and make rational choices. Thereafter, however, only the talented were to mount in varying degrees until the very talented, and only they, won the privilege of attending that favorite creation of his, the University of Virginia. I grant that the context of the problem of public education has radically altered since the eighteenth century, but I see no reason to alter his (or my) belief that higher education is a privilege for those who can understand it. I cannot find that Jefferson anywhere fell into the modern fallacy that professors are a sort of elegant intellectual butlers to be hired and fired as servants at the pleasure of students patronizing an academic motel. I am not skilled in political science, or social science, or psychiatry, or group therapy, but I cling to the historical truth that universities, when they succeed, have been places for the disinterested pursuit of truth. When they have failed—and I shall not

7

attempt to list the melancholy role of such failures in the Old World, the New World, Asia, and Africa—they have failed because they have become political bandstands or hospitals for the psychologically imbalanced.

I think the basis of any doctrine of rights and responsibilities, whether for Jew or Gentile, believer or atheist, is found in the great verse in Micah, which runs:

> What doth the Lord require of thee, but to do justly, and to love mercy, and to walk humbly with thy God?

This is not logical, it has no basis in political theory, and the agnostic and the atheist will have to deal with the words "Lord" and "God" as best they can. But do they prefer the logic of the rebels, thus described by Professor Herbert A. Deane of Columbia University in *Up Against the Ivy Wall*? *

> Again and again one is struck by the posture of complete self-righteousness and of unyielding moral absolutism in the attitudes and action of the radical leaders. "I am totally right and completely moral, and you—if you disagree with me—are absolutely wrong and completely wicked. Therefore there is no basis for any real discussion with you.". . . Faced with this complete moral certainty, one is tempted to cry out, in Cromwell's great phrase, "I beseech you, in the bowels of Christ, to think it possible you may be mistaken."

There is some reason to believe that Cromwell was somewhat more familiar with Micah than is Mr. Mark Rudd,

* By Jerry L. Avorn, Robert Friedman, and others, New York, 1968.

one of the student radicals, who also contributes to this volume.

Every age has its cant, and among the depressing cant terms of ours is the word "guilt." As an Ancient of Ancients, I am apparently supposed to share a feeling of guilt about the mess my contemporaries and I made of the world and of the republic. For individual sins of mine I have felt and still feel a considerable measure of remorse. Burke said he did not know how to indict a whole people, and I do not know how to condemn a whole generation. My contemporaries and I made a good many mistakes, but I am on the whole rather proud of our extraordinary record. Since under the doctrine of "relevance" the young do not know, and the younger academics do not find it necessary for them to know, any history as such, let me set down a few relevant facts. We fought, we sustained, we lived through two world wars, neither of them of our seeking, and unlike Germany, Italy, and Spain we preserved both the form and the content of republican government. We got through the depression of the 1930's, a depression that began in Europe though we had our share in that beginning, and we not only got through it, we got through it after the fashion of a responsible political democracy, neither sinking into the frowzy pseudo-financing of certain other countries, nor altering our belief in the long-run good sense of the American nation. With all its defects upon its head—and they are many—we preserved and increased the public education and enriched higher education. We developed great eleemosynary foundations. We altered the concept of big business from that of a soulless corporation to that of a responsible component of society, and in the decades when this amazing change took place, we improved, honestly administered, and honestly paid our taxes in a manner and to a degree beyond the comprehension of, let us say, a great many Frenchmen and Italians. We altered the whole course of American literature, we improved and enriched the relation between the arts in America and the American public, and we adapted or invented new forms of publication and communication. We greatly improved the status of woman in the United States, we diminished, though we did not eradicate, race and class prejudice, we softened the war, formerly bloody, between capital and labor, we laid firm foundations for the care of children, the sick, the poor, and the unemployed and unemployable. We began public housing. Above all, despite a famous protest march of the unemployed on Washington in the days of Herbert Hoover's presidency and various crowd protests here and there during the depression of the 1930's, usually against a foreclosure on farming property, we did not characteristically resort to mob violence as a brute weapon for change. We saw empires crumble around us—the Turkish, the Italian, the German, the British, the French, the Dutch among others —but we preserved the United States. It is also true that we created the radio, television, and modern advertising without sufficient public controls, and that we made the atom bomb. I have no excuse for our mismanagement of the first three, all of which are now used to drug judgment. I wish that atomic warfare had never been invented. But those who did not have to endure World War II and the preceding years, who did not have to experience the rape of cities, the ruin of countries, the slaughter of civilians, and the infernal murder factories of the Fascists and the Nazis cannot comprehend the desperation that, after Dunkirk and Pearl Harbor, made mere survival, or rather the survival of some fragment of the Western world, a far more paramount consideration

than, let us say, the abolition of college credit for the
ROTC; and, moreover, we have so far succeeded in controlling atomic destruction that no later bomb has been
dropped anywhere, and a great deal of atomic energy has
been put to peaceful use.

I suppose that for an Englishman to have lived
through the epoch of the French Revolution and the
Napoleonic wars was to have lived through a heroic
period of time. I think we oldsters who are so vocifer-
ously blamed for the woes of the world have the quiet
comfort of believing that, with all our faults, we lived up
to the measure of a heroic age.

But what has all this to do with humanism? I think
the crowning virtue of the humanities is that, properly
understood, properly taught, and properly studied, they
inculcate the long-range view. The long-range view
teaches wisdom. It teaches, among other things, that civic
violence mostly begets only counter-violence, that emotion is not policy, that adolescence is but a small part of
individual life, and that mankind, 99% of whose existence on this earth has been spent in the palaeolithic
period, progresses slowly and with uneven steps. Impatience and alienation cannot build or hold a state. Most
occupations are routine, and have to be, few jobs are
perpetually "interesting," a civilization of wandering is a
contradiction in terms, and against stupidity the gods
themselves are said to fight in vain. Nevertheless they
fight; the restless, who complain of a sterile culture,
ought to transplant themselves in imagination to the
steppes of Russia in the eighteenth century if they really
want to know what monotony is; our jobs, though routine, are now, as it were, embedded in so much leisure
time, individuality has more play than ever; and routine
occupations are giving way to machines except in those

areas where, believe it or not, the employed rather like routine. Changes for the better do sometimes succeed. But not even by the young can the normal flight of time and history be suddenly reversed or stopped so that a new, beautiful, planless and genial anarchy of equality, peace, drugs, and casual sexuality will dawn on some tomorrow, provided enough rebels band together to destroy government offices, universities, libraries, military depots, and courses of technical training for chemists, naval officers, military men, and secret agents.

I remarked some pages back that I put the word "generation" into quotation marks because I think its present use is an example of that false power by which we multiply distinctions. I question the validity of the assumption that the people of the United States, or of the world, fall neatly into two simple and antagonistic groups: (a) the young; and (b) everybody else. Human life is a continuum, now exhibiting a momentary increase in one age group, now in another; but these humps in the demographic curve tend by and by to straighten themselves out, as any mortality table will reveal. If I have complained of the conduct and arrogance of the young (and I have) I can remember a time when the sociological hotgospellers were haunted by a fear of the possible preponderance of the senile in our population. The young of course are at the moment unable to attribute any validity to the wisdom of their elders, however they may flock to psychiatrists, doctors, dentists, surgeons, a few favored philosophers well over thirty, and a library of books, many or most of which were not written when the authors were very young. Yet the ever going on of any culture (and ours will go on) depends upon the transmission of forms and values from one decade to another, allowance being made for improvement or decay. And after reading Crane Brinton's valuable *The Anatomy of Revolution* it is impossible to believe that any revolution attains its intended ends. After the English Civil Wars the English restored the monarchy. After the American Revolution the United States settled back upon a political pattern with a few exceptions so curiously like that of the mother country that intelligent observers began talking about the two democracies, the one crowned, the other republican. The conclusion of Tocqueville was that the government of France was centralized under Louis XIV, it remained centralized during the French Revolution and under Napoleon, and it continued to be centralized to his own day. It has remained centralized ever since. But rebels who refuse all tradition and all history and any wisdom to be drawn from history are doomed to repeat the mistakes in history—no brilliant observation of mine, for it goes back at least to Cicero.

If the crowning virtue of the humanities is that they teach, or should teach, the long-range view, the professional weakness of the humanities as taught in this country is that young humanists more and more confuse the liberal arts with the fine arts, intellectual maturation with self-expression (usually disguised as creativity), and true relevance with what is fashionably contemporary. I can not see that the wide, and as I think uncritical, acceptance of vaguely Freudian or vaguely Jungian modes of interpreting art is in any way yielding substantial values or nourishing that instinct for the permanent by which alone men can remain human. It is utterly naïve to think that even current art "reflects" life, more simplistic still to think that all art and all philosophy, past or present, have no other aim than thus to "reflect" the passing problem. To build a house for the humanities on the shifting interests and emotional drives of any single generation is to build it on sand. If one is a Christian, this is self-evident. If one is simply a theist, it is at least plausible. If one is an agnostic or an atheist it still makes sense. If one is an anarchist, it makes no sense because the anarchist will not even exclaim with Faust to some passing moment: "Tarry awhile! Thou art so fair." If the biologists talk about living in a post-Christian culture, humanism is not thereby denied. Consider Bertrand Russell's statement in "A Free Man's Worship" almost seventy years ago:

> A strange mystery it is that Nature, omnipotent but blind in the revolutions of her secular hurryings through the abysses of space, has brought forth at last a child, subject still to her power, but gifted with sight, with knowledge of good and evil, with the capacity of judging all the works of his unthinking Mother. In spite of Death, the mark and seal of parental control, Man is yet free, during his brief years, to examine, to criticize, to know, and in imagination to create. To him alone in the world with which he is acquainted, this freedom belongs; and in this lies his superiority to the resistless forces that control his outward life.

I do not see how the case for humanism and the case against anarchy can be more succinctly put, and I am against anarchy.

THE
HUMANITIES
IN
CIVILIZATION

VIOLENCE AND THE HUMANIST

WE LIVE in an era as brilliant and violent as the period
of the French Revolution. Within the memory of living
men there have been fought the Spanish-American War,
the Boer War, the Russo-Japanese War, four or five wars
in the Balkans, World War I, World War II, the Korean
War, the war in Vietnam, and the Six-Day War between
Israel and the Arab states. We have lived through a
bloody revolution in Russia and its counter-revolutions,
purges, and massacres, two revolutions in Italy, two in
Germany (one the most fearful in modern history), two
or three or four in China, and innumerable less spectacu-
lar revolts in the Balkan countries, Turkey, Poland, Austria, Spain, Portugal, France, Hungary, Algeria, India,
what was once French Indo-China, the Dutch East In-
dies, Egypt, most of Africa outside Egypt, and virtually
all the Latin-American republics.

New nations have been created, sometimes on no ascer-
tainable principle, in numbers that burden the memory
and clog the United Nations. Many new countries and
some old ones seem unable to exist except in a state of

"Violence and the Humanist" was the annual Samuel S. Strat-
ton Lecture at Middlebury College, delivered October 2, 1967. It
was first published in pamphlet form by the college.

17

tension with their neighbors—the Arab countries against Israel, Pakistan against India, Cuba against the rest of the New World, contemporary China against every other country except Rumania and Albania. If one looks for areas that have remained peaceful since 1890, one is hard put to it to go beyond Sweden and Switzerland. We have also witnessed the collapse of the League of Nations; and some prophesy the disintegration of the United Nations because of the cumbersomeness of its structure and because a numerically tiny minority of its members retain an absolute veto power.

Other elements in the situation, at once dismal and dramatic, worry us all. One is the extraordinary bitterness of religious and racial animosity—Arab against Jew, Oriental against European, black men against white men. This last has twisted the history of the Union of South Africa out of all semblance to the representative republic dreamed of by General Smuts and in the United States has led to race riots that have the character of civil wars.

Partly as a function of racism, partly as a function of nationalism (that vast and powerful emotion let loose on the world by the romantic movement), we have also witnessed the dissolution of empires—the Austro-Hungarian, the British, the French, the German, the Dutch, the Italian and, despite loud cries of being misunderstood, that of the United States, which has given independence to Cuba and the Philippines, dominion status to Puerto Rico, and statehood to Alaska and Hawaii.

Another troubling force is the Malthusian predicament. World population pushes steadily against the means of sustaining life, the world's food supply is inequitably distributed, and water, too often polluted by sewage or industrial waste, is in short supply. Population pressures also create problems in great cities from India

18

to America—slums, ignorance, poverty, disease, crime, prejudice, filth, a rising resentment against somebody or something not defined. A minor but distressing aspect of municipal malaise is the appearance in the younger generation of beatniks, hippies, and teeny-boppers resentful of cultural sterility, who go all out to deny standard values—they riot in China and boast of taking drugs in the United States. Over all hangs the threat of atomic destruction. Many observers think there was prescience in the statement of H. G. Wells that the future is a race between education and catastrophe. This is the world in which the humanist like the rest of us has to live.

Contemporary culture is characterized by specialism and mechanization. I pass over the resulting disturbance of an ancient relation between nature and man, pass over likewise the question whether by inventing more complicated machines, we may end by enslaving mankind, and note that to manage modern life, we increasingly rely upon specialization. The humanist is not in this sense expert. He has no competence in science; and Lord Snow is not alone in wondering whether the split between science and the humanities may not prove a disaster. The humanist is not a statesman. He has no training in economics, sociology, anthropology, social psychology, or psychiatry. His area is the general history of thought, culture, philosophy, and the arts. Unless he is a professional philosopher, he takes his philosophy at second hand, and borrows what he knows about formal religion from the divinity schools. Of course when he specializes —say, in structural linguistics or baroque painting—he exhibits the qualities and defects of any other specialist— zeal for limited knowledge and a tendency to minimize everything outside his field. But just as the mathematician denies that mathematics is arid and acclaims it as one of the noblest achievements of the mind, so the humanist has a right to be judged, not by the mythical pedant who counted the final e's in Chaucer, but by figures like Plato, Erasmus, and Emerson. Unfortunately, though we respond with fervor to personalized nobility in a man like John Fitzgerald Kennedy, abstract pleas of noble intention are viewed with suspicion.

The humanist's concern is with art, religion, philosophy, and history; that is, with systems of value and patterns of organized perceptiveness. Understandably his feelings are somewhat mixed when he contemplates some of the productions of art, religion, and philosophy and the uses (or misuses) to which they have been put. A simple instance is the vogue of Thoreau's "Essay on Civil Disobedience," said to have inspired Gandhi in India and the civil rights marches in the United States. He notes however, that both these movements ended in violence, which in turn produced counter-violence, one of the ironies of recent history being that the Student Non-Violent Co-ordinating Committee is now led by persons who preach violence as a mode of getting what they want. The philosophy of Hegel and the music dramas of Wagner are in some sense the matrices out of which the Nazi movement was born; it is useless to protest that Hegel never intended anything like genocide or that with all his anti-semitism on his head Wagner wrote his masterpieces from *The Flying Dutchman* through the *Ring* to *Parsifal* to celebrate triumphal love. A succession of paintings running from the *trompe l'oeil* works of the baroque period to the surrealistic masterpieces of Salvador Dali have become the excuse and the occasion of so-called psychedelic art, that frank celebrant of sensation rather than pattern, which substitutes intensity for lasting form. Music profits from the invention of new instruments and the use of new systems of tonality; it is, however, difficult to see that the banging of bongo drums, the casualness of electronic noises, and the fortissimo playing of rock-and-roll does more than teeter on the edge of brinkmanship in a world already too full of noises. As for religion, Dr. Leary apparently regards himself as the founder of a new one.

The humanist is neither a scientist nor a social scientist; yet in this situation he has some modest claim to be heard. If he has no scientific or social formula to stop race riots, subdue nationalism, improve the food supply, or persuade a fraction of misguided youth that there is no visible virtue in dirty feet, what can he say? He is in the main a synthesizer. Possibly a bit of synthesis, though it will cure nothing, will at least give us a chance for reflection.

Professionally the humanist has, I think, three important concerns: he is devoted to language as language; he believes in rationality; and he clings to the historical point of view. Let me, then, attempt a bit of synthesizing. It will not be exciting, it will not reform anything, it will present no program, but it may occasion thought.

I begin with language. Let us, said Dr. Johnson, rid our minds of cant. Cant refers to the use of stock phrases temporarily in fashion, and makes people think they think. The age of advertising and of self-advertising goes beyond earlier times in its addiction to stock phrases. Let me illustrate by one very simple and one more complicated example.

A silly slogan that has had vogue among some of the younger generation is the injunction: "Don't trust anybody over thirty." Because it is both silly and characteristic, the sentence is worth analyzing. In the first place, though drawing a line at eighteen or twenty-one might make some vague political sense, an arbitrary arithmetical division makes no sense at all. Why thirty? Why not twenty-six, or seventeen, or forty-five? In the second place this same younger generation trusts a great many persons over thirty—parents, who send them money every month; physicians, to whom they repair when taken ill; park attendants, when they play their flutes and guitars; and writers and leaders like Kahlil Gibran. In the third place, since in a very few years this same generation will be thirty or older, it follows logically that they must then distrust both themselves and their contemporaries and be in turn distrusted.

The second case is more complicated. The country is divided over the morality and the policy of our war in Vietnam, and liberals and newspaper men have invented the phrase "credibility gap" to indicate their distrust of the President. Emotion grows by what it feeds on. A month before this lecture was given a liberal magazine entitled its leading article: "The White House Lies," meaning that the President of the United States and his administrative assistants are habitual liars. Part of the second paragraph of this article reads: "It is a new idea to Americans—the idea that the Government lies to them—and one that does not go down easily. It runs counter to the American grain." The paragraph also states: "We have seen the Government become attuned to falsehood as a routine way of conducting its affairs, to the point where hardly a day passes without producing its own challenge to credulity."

Without any commitment on the war, let me examine this doctrine. In the first place no government can long exist that is wholly attuned to lies. In the second place there is no way of proving either the truth or the falsity of this sweeping condemnation, which would include the

22

Department of Commerce, the Treasury, the Post-Office, the Coast and Geodetic Survey, the Department of Health, Education, and Welfare, the Federal courts, the Department of Agriculture, the Social Security and Medicare programs, Federal aid to housing, welfare, agriculture, education, wounded veterans, and much else in the excoriation. Few, I think, would agree that all these branches of government are attuned to falsehood; and in fact the statement does not mean what it says. It means only the President of the United States, his public relations officers, the Secretary of State, the Secretary of Defence, and, I suppose, some members of Congress (I doubt the writers would condemn the entire Congress as liars) seem to be habitual tellers of falsehoods.

Undoubtedly there are hypocrisy and prevarication in government, and I do not deny that this may be true of the Johnson administration. It is to be observed, however, that in a world of violent flux, what seemed true in January may prove to be totally wrong in June; that a great American once said that a foolish consistency is the hobgoblin of little minds; that there is at least a possibility that a White House spokesman may be misinformed, mistaken, or injudicious without therefore being a Machiavelli; and, finally, that in fielding questions asked by newspaper men who are sometimes more interested in trapping the respondent into damaging admissions than they are in dispassionate statement, the White House representative is forced to choose between the need of concealing what a hostile world should not know and the necessity of somehow retaining good relations with a hostile reporter.

Moreover, occupants of the White House (or its equivalent) have usually been charged with deceit, fraud, or immorality. After leaving the presidency George Washington wrote that he had been "abused in such exaggerated and indecent terms as could scarcely be applied to a Nero, a notorious defaulter, or even a common pickpocket." Here is an example: "If ever a nation was debauched by a man," wrote the editor of *The Aurora,* a newspaper of 1798, "the American nation has been debauched by Washington." John Adams, it seems, wanted to turn America into a monarchy, in anticipation of which he sent General Pinckney to England aboard a frigate to procure four pretty girls as mistresses, two for the general, two for the President. Andrew Jackson was called a liar, a thief, a drunkard, a Negro trader, a bigamist, an adulterer, a cockfighter, insane, ignorant, cruel, and bloodthirsty. In 1864 supporters of McClellan, Lincoln's opponent, denounced the martyr President as a filthy story-teller, a despot, a secessionist, a liar, a thief, a braggart, a buffoon, a usurper, a monster, an ignoramus, an old scoundrel, a perjurer, a robber, a swindler, a tyrant, a fiend, a land-pirate, a "long, lean, lank, lantern-jawed, high-cheek-boned, spavined, rail-splitting stallion." Lincoln's successor, Andrew Johnson, was accused of being privy to Lincoln's assassination. In our time Franklin D. Roosevelt was characterized as the "Machiavellian Chief of the New Deal," a man who sought the destruction of constitutional government and was moving towards despotism through a fog of lies and immorality. He displayed, it was alleged, the symptoms of encephalomyelitis—"uncontrollable laughter," "attacks of excitement with wild laughing, and of depression and high suggestibility." He was poisoned by a Russian waiter at Teheran, using curare, a deadly alkaloid, poisoned all over again at Yalta, and poisoned a third time apparently with arsenic, since at Warm Springs the body "turned black in four hours." In 1939 "no one reposes the slightest

24

dependence in the good faith [of the government's] agents, employees or its officers."

If violent language like these examples strikes us as hysterical, it is at least possible that similar language is hysterical now. I do not say that the occupants of the White House have been uniformly candid; I do say, first, that charges of lying and immorality have been leveled at a good many presidents; and, second, that those who know no history are bound to repeat history.

It may be argued that a silly slogan and an excited article by two newspaper men should not be taken with solemn seriousness. Perhaps not. Style, however, is the morality of language. Our language is too often the language of violence, and those who employ it to complain of or expose the immorality of a violent society contribute to the immorality they complain of. American advertising offers a thousand instances of this verbal violence. Here, for example, is part of an advertisement for a recent novel by a writer said to be a practicing psychologist who combines "professional study of human motivations" "with a fast-paced writing style." What this last means I do not know. The novel concerns a "quiet town" that "exploded in a chain reaction of horror and shame when the war hero returned from Vietnam and killed the person he loved most; when his kid brother romanced his steady while having an affair with her mother; when all values crumbled and respectability vanished in a morass of hypocrisy and scandal." To the judicious the book thus epitomized would seem to be a rather imperfect picture of human motivations. The language of the advertisement is vulgar and violent ("his kid brother romanced his steady," "all values crumbled and respectability vanished in a morass of hypocrisy and scandal"), and the author's "fast-paced style," if advertising is indicative, must be violent also.

This advertisement is not unusual. I pick out at random from a single issue of the *New York Times Book Review* three other advertisements for books. One concerns a "tall, dashingly handsome" hero who is "every bit as fiendish as his ancestors"; one is a "profound female confession" and the third, which concerns a book on surf-riding, promises that if I read it, I will "come out the end as jazzed—and stocked—and pumped—and unplugged as the hero." It is instructive to compare the tone of advertising in a popular medium with that in magazines like the *Scientific American* or the *New England Journal of Medicine*. Let us not complain if a segment of the population seeks excitement in drugs, sexuality, or cynicism. Advertising paid for by responsible business men, whether of books or bleaches, automobiles or underclothing, teaches them that life is perpetual ecstasy.

The style spreads. Thus a senator of the United States admired by the liberals signs an article stating that the great society is a sick society, "sick" being used in its curious modern sense of depraved. If true, the indictment is overwhelming. But is it true? A much publicized social commentator is touted as being "on the side of the people against a stagnant government . . . a dehumanizing industrial and scientific complex . . . [and] self-serving interests." Who would not be? But the statement is filled with question-begging epithets. An educational experiment at Fordham is publicized as "complete freedom" for thirteen men and seventeen women students, something no one has experienced since Adam and Eve, and even they had at least one important prohibition. But each student in this experiment "is looking for his own coherent center from which to branch out into interconnected studies." Professor Leslie Fiedler of the University of

Buffalo, recently arrested and charged with possessing marijuana, would, I suspect, object to having his case tried in the newspapers before he appears in court, but he has now tried his own case in the *New York Review of Books* and brings in a verdict of innocence on the ground that his primary responsibility as a teacher "is to be free and to provide a model of freedom for the young." I do not know that being charged with possessing marijuana is being a model of freedom, but I would stoutly argue to the contrary and declare that the primary freedom of the teacher is to assume responsibility and to teach that there is no freedom without it. In the words of a great, if conservative, English poet

Me this unchartered freedom tires.

Violent words have as little morality as violent actions.

There are two strong, though mutually contradictory, answers to my critique. The first is that it doesn't matter what we print because we are going to rid ourselves of linear writing and therefore linear printing. I think this is the drift of Marshall McLuhan's *Understanding Media,* but I do not pretend to understand Marshall McLuhan. It is plainly the drift of an interview given by a French archaeologist, who has the misfortune to express himself clearly. In a recent issue of *Réalités* M. André Leroi-Gourhan, author of *Le Geste et la Parole* (1966), declared that linear writing is a recent phenomenon in the history of man and that progress will quickly eliminate it. Writing and, I infer, printing are losing ground to the telephone, the dictaphone, and audio-visual media. This disappearance will be a good thing because linear writing forces thought to flow in a mere one-dimensional frame of reference that impoverishes thinking. Our author says the consequences of giving up linear writing will be less serious for science than for literature and philosophy, modes of expression that must be completely recast in the future. Then comes this ominous sentence: "I might add that in any case a multi-dimensional system permits a much better use of men's irrational faculties than linear writing does." I am not persuaded that I want man's irrational faculties to operate in any more dimensions than they now use; and so far as liberty of expression is concerned, it is obvious there is far less of it on the radio and television and over the telephone than there is in print. Of course pre-historians move through majestic arcs of time, but I feel that M. Leroi-Gourhan's notion that linear writing will soon disappear requires some correction. Writing and printing will be with us for a long time to come. This academic absolutism seems to me to be an example of academic cant.

The second argument is far more cogent. Having begun by saying that ours is an age of brilliance and of violence, I cannot complain if we have both glitter and brutality expressed in substance and style. Literature, it is argued, is a mirror of society; and, moreover, empirical observation, recent history, and sound psychological theory teach us that man is essentially irrational, erotic, and motivated by such primitive drives as the death-wish, sadism, and utter self-regard.

Moreover, not only current fiction and drama but most of the leading fictionists of the last fifty years are novelists of violence. The great American dramatist of the twentieth century is Eugene O'Neill, and nobody pretends that plays like *Desire Under the Elms, The Emperor Jones,* and *Mourning Becomes Electra* are drawing-room comedies. It is but a step from O'Neill's violence to the theater of the absurd. Fiction and the drama are also consonant with the so-called blow-in-the-eye fashion in

architecture, the distortion in sculpture, and the dehu-
manization of painting evident in efforts through the
energy of pigment to catch the predominant qualities of a
mechanical age. I have already spoken of music. We
want noise, action, size. The trend is irreversible.

I shall not pause on the point that only history is
irreversible and that trends are frequently reversed, but I
shall strengthen the adversary argument still further. Not
only do modern masters of fiction make violence their
theme, but literary violence has been with us a long time.
An able historian of homicide as a topic for the imagination, Professor David B. Davis of Cornell, in an article
published last year in the *Annals of the American Academy of Political and Social Science,* pointed out that from
its birth the American novel has been fascinated by
crime. Obvious examples are *Wieland, The Marble Faun,
A Connecticut Yankee in King Arthur's Court,* and *An
American Tragedy.* He notes the considerable amount of
carnage in the world's classics from Homer to Dostoiev-
ski. Strip the plays of Shakespeare of style and thought:
what you have left is unbelievable melodrama and incredible farce. At the end of *Hamlet* the stage is strewn with
corpses. Half way through the drama Macbeth declares:

> I am in blood
> Stepp'd in so far, that, should I wade no more,
> Returning were as tedious as go o'er.

Of the eleven main characters in *King Lear* eight are
taken off by violent means before the play concludes, and
the tragedy is, moreover, stuffed with treachery, ingrati-
tude, bastardy, deceit, torture, injustice, thunder and
lightning, battle, parental curses, pretended madness, and
real insanity. The purport of the story seems to be
summed up in two famous passages:

As flies to wanton boys, so are we to the gods—
They kill us for their sport;

and

Men must endure
Their going hence, even as their coming hither;
Ripeness is all.

This is scarcely optimism.

No one, however, has suggested that this great and terrible play is a mirror of life in London or in Stratford in 1606, even though murder and other crimes were not unknown under James I. There would seem to be something wrong with the simple doctrine that art mirrors life. The one Shakespearean play that richly reflects contemporary living is in fact *The Merry Wives of Windsor,* a piece so jolly it is the basis of the greatest comic opera of the nineteenth century. Which is the mirror—*King Lear?* Or *Merry Wives?* Shakespeare got his theater of violence from foreign sources and chronicles of old, unhappy, far-off things and battles long ago. They pleased audiences then, and they have pleased audiences since, not, I think, because they were images of Jacobean violence, nor even symbols of that violence. What sets them apart from contemporary accounts, say, of attempts to murder Queen Elizabeth, is a way of looking at the whole of human life and of reflecting upon it, not merely reflecting it. Literature is not transcript but interpretation.

But if our age is violent, if our literature is violent also, and if that literature is not a simple mirror-image of contemporary disorder, why, then, the curious parallelism? Mr. Davis rightly says that critics who interpret violence in contemporary writing as symptomatic of a sick society are wrong. I agree. The question is not quantitative and sociological, but qualitative, philosophical, and aesthetic. Mr. Davis's explanation is that American writers are now trying to synthesize the rebelliousness of antirationalism with an older native tradition of the individualistic hero; for example, Cooper's Leatherstocking and the Virginian in Owen Wister's Western novel. These heroes had to prove themselves by activity. An extreme case in the other direction would be, I suppose, Richard Wright's powerful novel, *Native Son* (1940), in which Bigger Thomas causelessly and brutally murders a white girl and a black girl. I think there is truth in Mr. Davis's observation, but I think one must go a little deeper.

Leatherstocking and the Virginian faintly resemble the Shakespearian hero. Like Hamlet or Macbeth they are caught in a conflict of codes—Leatherstocking between the code of the wilderness and a Christian upbringing, the Virginian between the mores of the West and the mores of the East. Neither denies that codes exist. Bigger Thomas, however, shrugs off all codes as hypocritical except hypocrisy and in so doing he is supposed to illustrate the plight of the Negro. The shock value of the book on first reading is great, but the impact is one of horror rather than of pity and understanding. One critic, to be sure, avers that *Native Son* shows us the transformation of self-destructive rage into art, but this, or so it seems to me, is precisely what it does not show; what we have is a record of a violent man committing violent acts and using violent words, as, indeed, the author does also. Dorothy Canfield Fisher, who admired the book, innocently revealed the root of the difficulty when she wrote: "*Native Son* is the first report in fiction we have had from those who succumb to the distracting cross-currents of contradictory nerve-impulses, from those whose behavior patterns give evidence of the same bewildered, senseless tangle of abnormal nerve-reactions studied in animals by psychologists in laboratory experiments." Precisely. But let us not confuse the value of a case history, which is great, with the illuminating power of imagination conveyed through style, which is greater.

Style is a way of looking, of estimating, of valuing, which creates a psychological distance between the thing viewed or written about or heard, and the viewer, the reader, or the listener. Style really makes a difference. I can translate the original of the story of the Gadarene swine and the awe Jesus inspired by the simple statement: "Everybody around there asked him to get out of here." The King James translation runs: "the whole multitude of the Gadarenes round about besought him to depart from them." Is there no difference between these universes of discourse? I can let myself overhear one young man say, "God, am I bored!" and another say:

> How weary, stale, flat, and unprofitable
> Seem to me all the uses of this world.

Do the sentences connote the same values? The initial shock of certain four-letter words in print had, doubtless, a certain value. Now they are simply dull words like worn dimes, their only meaning being either that they reduce certain human actions to physiological mechanisms or that they reproduce the empty language employed at certain social levels, leaving the reader to impute to speaker or writer a meaning that isn't there. Does it make no difference how we talk and write? Animalism and automatism logically mean the end of art.

Nor can it be argued that an age of panel discussions, dialogs, symposiums, meet-the-press programs, interviews, political commentators, subliminal persuaders, and universal TV sets lacks a burning interest in words. The same world which admires the oral skill of a Franklin Roosevelt, a Winston Churchill and a John F. Kennedy, was appalled by the oratorical hypnotism of Hitler, and watches communist propaganda with apprehension. We cannot shrug off style as a problem of no consequence. We are not to speak blank verse or deliver the Gettysburg Address, but we ought to believe that the most imbecile way to control violence is to multiply both fuzzy expressions and violent words.

But as not every one will agree that style is thus basic, I turn to the other half of the problem; namely, the doctrine that man is essentially irrational, erotic, sadistic, and primitive, given over to self-hatred, the death-wish, alienation, and a dull or frantic egotism. Many moderns regard the proposition as self-evident. True, it curiously resembles statements by authors like Swift, Jonathan Edwards, Schopenhauer, Nietzsche, George Sorel, and others, but the revelation is felt to come in its full force to the twentieth century, negating all sublime theories that man is potentially rational, noble, and just.

Advocates of this view have a very strong case. They point out that after centuries of religion man seems as stupid and bestial as ever. They cite the slaughter of the Jews and the horrors of modern warfare; they cite our slums, our crime waves, our business and political dishonesty, fakery in the art world, and hypocrisy in publishing; they cite the dissipation of such ancient controls as that of the family and the church, the school and the home. They justify civil disobedience and cultural indifference, moral lassitude and a retreat into never-never lands of dream or nightmare as the inevitable consequence of the wide hold this view of human nature has obtained.

Once when Ellen Glasgow's novels were not selling as

well as they should, her publisher, Nelson Doubleday, said to her: "Ellen, what you ought to do is to write an optimistic novel about the West." To this Miss Glasgow replied: "Nelson, if there's anything I know less about than the West, it's optimism." In my observation attempts to define, delimit, or controvert the charge that modern man has made a mess of culture are commonly negated by the counter-assertion that to see anything else in life is just so much silly optimism. I do not wish to incur the grave charge of being an optimist. Historical comparisons will not remove the terror under which many of us live, nor do I wish to minimize the viciousness in man or in society. Nevertheless I shall try at least to delimit and perhaps to controvert the extremist assumption, commonly called existentialist by those who have misunderstood Kierkegaard and Sartre, that man is so fundamentally forlorn and wrong, we might as well recognize the fact and be done with it.

In the first place the hurt that one feels about anarchy and evil would not be possible unless one had had, intellectually prior to this sorrow, some apprehension of the nature of order, rationality, loveliness, and calm. Chaos cannot know chaos. Even Satan in *Paradise Lost* knew justice and peace before he, ruining, fell, to experience the torments

Both of lost happiness and lasting pain.

Almost all religions and almost all philosophies have held that whatever the present depraved condition of mankind may be, men are capable of rising on stepping stones of their dead selves to higher things. Phrases about lost Edens and lost innocence imply that there were innocence and Eden to lose. This may of course all be sheer illusion, and nothing is more painful than lost illusions.

34

This in turn is emotionally true, but the question still remains: how did the illusion get established in the first place? and this is followed by a second question: why should the twentieth century alone have possession of disillusioned psychological truth?

In the second place, were the doctrine really true, the groups that proclaim it—the novelists, the poets, the anti-war groups, the anti-draft groups, the anti-culture groups, in fact all the groups that protest the power of the state and deny the validity of its laws—would shortly dissolve. For if hypocrisy, evil, selfishness, and destructive drives are universal human traits, why are a happy few here and there exempt from what they claim to be the universal condition of mankind? No group, however disillusioned, can, if one admits the major premise, long survive. Obviously, however, groups do survive. Rebels cheerfully cooperate with each other on principles, however ghostly, of honor, loyalty, and esteem. One can of course fall back on the doctrine of the saving remnant, but when a group announces that it, and it alone, is the saving remnant, the majority of men are somehow not instantly convinced.

The weaknesses of men and the imperfections of life have long troubled saints and sages. I read that "man is born unto trouble, as the sparks fly upward." I read also: "I have seen all the works that are done under the sun; and, behold, all is vanity and vexation of spirit." "Never to have been born," runs a famous chorus in Sophocles, "is much the best; and the next best, by far, is to return by the speediest way where our beginnings are." "We have just enough religion to make us hate," wrote Swift, "but not enough to make us love one another." A more modern writer, once fashionable but now fallen into disfavor, declared in a memorable quatrain:

35

The troubles of our proud and angry dust
    Are from eternity and shall not fail.
Bear them we can, and if we can we must.
    Shoulder the sky, my lad, and drink your ale.*

The same poet, whose stoicism makes more sense than the rhetoric of the very angry very young men, wrote also his "Epitaph on an Army of Mercenaries":

These, in the day when heaven was falling,
    The hour when earth's foundations fled,
Followed their mercenary calling,
    And took their wages and are dead.

Their shoulders held the skies suspended;
    They stood, and earth's foundations stay;
What God abandoned, these defended,
    And saved the sum of things for pay.*

Saving the sum of things for pay may not be saintly or heroic motivation but it is at least a step or so above anarchy and negation. Even William Faulkner, whose plots more often involve violence than not, held that man will prevail, and by man he did not mean people like the Snopes family.

The doctrine that man, notably modern man, is motivated wholly or principally by irrationalism and primitive urges simply will not wash. Doubtless the Age of the Enlightenment had romantic notions about the presence of reason in all humanity; this age, however, seems to

* Permission to quote these four lines from "The Chestnut Casts His Flambeaux" and the poem "Epitaph on an Army of Mercenaries," both by A. E. Housman, has been granted by Holt, Rinehart and Winston, Inc., New York, and The Society of Authors, London, the latter acting as representative for the Estate of the author and for Jonathan Cape Ltd., London. Holt, Rinehart and Winston, Inc., and Jonathan Cape Ltd. are publishers of *Collected Poems of A. E. Housman.*

have equally romantic misconceptions about unreason. Consider some of the accomplishments of rationality. The vast structure of our brilliant scientific patterns—astronomy, biology, chemistry, geology, mathematics, and a score of other disciplines—is created, maintained, and advanced by responsible intellectuals. So is our enormous medical progress, including the alleviation or cure of scores of diseases formerly thought incurable, the care we give to children and the aging, and our concern for the health of the poor. There are deficiencies, and bad ones; for example, babies born in the slums or in poverty-stricken rural areas do not receive the attention they ought to have. But to make this deficiency the measure of our modern concern is to make the part do duty for the whole. A hundred years ago the mortality rate for all babies was so high it now seems to us incredible. Our concern for public health here and abroad, still unequal to the task, nevertheless diminishes the impact of disease. Our technological patterns are the products of rational skill in applying scientific principles to brute matter. We take for granted our system of interchangeable parts; but if you have ever lived in a country where interchangeable parts form no element in the economy, you will discover the value of what we take for granted. One may justly complain of those insolent chariots, the automobiles, and of their manufacturers, complain also of the imperviousness of politicians and highway engineers to simple domestic values and to beauty, but does anybody really want to go back to the ox-cart? The airplane is as wonderful as the pyramids. We move fearlessly up and down in our amazing elevators. We clothe most of our population cheaply, economically, and easily—think back to the time when the sewing-woman came to spend a week in the house to make and repair clothes. I hold no brief for

37

packaged foods; nevertheless they are sanitary and wholesome. Only when you have eaten in other countries notorious for potential food poisoning do you realize the American accomplishment. I grant we have polluted the air, the rivers, and the ocean shores, but we have also created programs for the scientific control of pollution. We are told that our urban civilization breeds mainly discontent. It breeds discontent, as did our agrarian culture, but you have only to watch thousands upon thousands moving with relative comfort from the cities to parks, fishing streams, ocean beaches, wilderness areas, camp sites, and ski resorts to learn that our urban civilization is also preserving the wilderness as agrarian culture did not, and this despite the opposition of contemporary vested interests. Finally, in quite another field, our legal system, complicated, cumbersome and often infuriating, is, oddly enough, admired and imitated abroad.

At this point it is proper for all right-minded sensibilitists—a word I owe to Robert Frost—to say that I sound either like Macaulay or the local boosters' club. The business point of view is of course limited. Limited also is that of the economist, the sociologist, the engineer, the scientist, the doctor, and the politician. A mere calculus of probability would therefore lead us to infer that the writer's point of view and the humanist's point of view may be limited also. Emerson once remarked that he saw no reason to suppose librarians are wiser than other men.

It would take me far afield to argue that a literary interpretation, penetrating though it often is and large as its scope may sometimes be, is limited also. I am afraid that literary pundits are sometimes curiously inconsistent. The critic, writer, or scholar who would not dream of accepting James Thompson's dark masterpiece, *The City of Dreadful Night,* as a total view of Victorian spirituality will enthusiastically inform his classes or his readers that *The Waste-Land* is a full and trustworthy picture of the spiritual aridity of modern life. Both works are powerful, each is a haunting presentation of personalized philosophy, and that philosophy expresses values that a sensitive minority finds persuasive. Meanwhile the churches enrich or comfort the lives of thousands (both poems appeal to the church), an altruistic longing for a better society drives other thousands forward on various programs of amelioration, and the same younger generation that condemns the academic world as banal, regimented, and tyrannical fights to get into the colleges and universities it condemns.

Reform movements commonly exhibit the wildness of a crusade. Iconoclasm is always more exciting than analysis. The humanist has made many mistakes, the worst being his contemporary tendency to misinterpret the past in terms of the present tense, but at his best he clings to two terms: patience and responsibility. They are not a program. They are only guides. And he concludes, or I conclude for him, with three general observations:

First, the celebration of freedom as the only ethical absolute is self-defeating as Mr. Justice Holmes long ago pointed out; and were it to become the principal agency of social action, would end in either anarchy or despotism. Second, the celebration of violence either as an end in itself or as a short-cut to political or social change can only end, unless all history is in error, in the disruption of order and of culture. Third, the celebration of irrationality as a primary value is not only a one-sided view of the accomplishments of man, but must end by superseding itself. Man may not be a wholly rational animal, but even Swift described him as a being capable of reason, and, like Sigmund Freud and Carl Jung, believed that the reason of man should govern his irrational instincts. Such is, or should be, the creed of the humanist. I think it is.

39

THE ARTS IN A WORLD OF SCIENCE

B̲ERTRAND R̲USSELL once remarked that in higher mathematics we do not know what we are doing nor why we are doing it. As I contemplate the vast, vague question before me—what is the future of the arts in a world of science?—I am reminded of his statement. Why is it assumed that the future is going to be a world of science? This is sheer pride, like that of Ozymandias—

> on the pedestal these words appear:
> "My name is Ozymandias, king of kings:
> Look on my works, ye Mighty, and despair!"
> . . . Round the decay
> Of that colossal wreck, boundless and bare
> The lone and level sands stretch far away.

The total triumph of science at some future time has been announced on several occasions in world history, but such

This essay was my contribution to a symposium upon the future of the arts in a world of science held at the Massachusetts Institute of Technology in commemorating its centennial in 1961. Under the title "What Science Can Never Do" it was printed in *The Graduate Journal* in the winter of 1963.

40

science as we have is at the mercy of politics, a decline of population, war, and the alternating beat of Yin and Yang, since, as Toynbee says, "Creation would not be creative if it did not swallow up all things in itself, including its own opposite." For science history is an enemy to be vanquished, full of false theories and bad reasoning; for art, history, including even the end of history, is substance itself. The dream of a scientific triumph in a world that is perpetually tomorrow seems to me as childlike as the dream of a Golden Age.

But if we suppose the future lies with science, are there to be no scientists? Or are machines to beget scientism for its own queer sake? If there are scientists, they will live, laugh, hate, marry, beget children, retire and die, even as we. Since art finds its meaning in laughter, tears, joy, sorrow, hope, awe, passion, regret, the fear of death, and the hatred of old age, human emotions and the specificity of individual values—what happens, happens to me, not to you—the themes will continue that shaped the *Iliad* and Ray Bradbury's *The Martian Chronicles,* an Aegean sheep-herding tune and the Concord Sonata of Charles Ives, a plastic marl statue from the neolithic near Jericho and the sculpture of Epstein. The incommensurability of the way of science and the way of art forces the thoughtful soul into declaring that the question implicit in the topic is something that really begs the question.

If, however, the problem is: how shall art deal with science? everything depends upon what one means by science. Does this term include pure science only, or does it refer to pure science, applied science, the philosophy of science, technology and engineering, medicine and psychology, and perhaps even the pseudo-science I find in advertising? So far as pseudo-science unfortunately shapes culture, pseudo-art will be content with it and genuine art will continue to attack pseudo-science. So far as medicine and psychology are good things, they are good in themselves, but I find nothing in the history of art to show that a mastery of any psychological systems leads *per se* to the creation by painter, poet, novelist, sculptor, or musician of memorable characters, and much to show that memorable imaginary beings from Shakespeare's Cleopatra to George F. Babbitt come into existence without benefit of psychology or medicine in the modern sense. So far as applied science creates new things, art will deal with them as it has dealt with the invention of the boat or the creation of television; it will refer them to the passions and motives of men. If the question refers to some fancied extension of human life in time or space, as when we say that medical care increases the life-span or that undreamed-of vehicles will take us to other planets, the arts will continue to operate in terms of youth, maturity, old age, and death, in terms of love, hate, awe, fear, reverence, and pity; and since not even science offers any immediate prospect of abolishing time, space, and mortality, we may confidently believe that old age as pictured in Ecclesiastes or Maximian, dissatisfaction as portrayed in *Hamlet* or *Faust,* the mystery of death as embodied in Saint Gaudens' statue at Rock Creek, and the ambivalence of triumph set forth in the *Eroica*—these or their future equivalents will continue to do what science can never do.

Theorists, of course—a Jeremy Bentham or a John B. Watson, a Condillac or a Marquis de Sade—will always argue that a simple stimulus-response correlation is at the basis of action, but this is not science, only assumption; and art, meanwhile, forever subtle, eludes this simplicistic theory and continues to demonstrate that meaning is more than the sum of its parts. The problem of free will and determinism is not a scientific question, but if it were, art has the same interest in determination of the will that she has in universal gravitation—so much and no more. The world exists, objects come and go, men appear and vanish, and after many a summer dies the swan. Her interest is in record and beauty, in the great puzzle of what, out of vanity, we call the human predicament. I do not know what philosophy was embraced by the builders of the Parthenon, but whether they were determinists or idealists, sceptics or believers, the evening lights still play over the fluted columns and the evening shadows punctually appear in that great ruin with every sunset. Lever House in New York is fancier engineering (or is it?) and wastes less space, but whether it is more or less beautiful as architecture is not a problem of science, even though one may properly speak of solving equations elegantly and of a beautiful operation for lung cancer.

True it is that scientific theory and scientific investigations have in the past touched imagination into expressive art form. Our evidence is nevertheless scanty, so that, even though we know how the telescope stirred seventeenth-century poets, we do not know how the imagination was stirred by that earlier and even more dazzling invention, the wheel. Most sensitive persons would grant, I think, that Polynesian songs celebrating a swift outrigger canoe are better poetry than metropolitan verse celebrating an airplane. It is likewise obvious that the expressiveness of Beethoven is in some degree a function of the larger ensemble of scientifically tuned instruments available to him, since a Beethoven symphony would have been impossible under Augustus Caesar. But this, again, is to substitute substance for mode; and the fact that Europe has produced no second Æschylus is no argument for the revival of the complexities of the Greek language, but

43

only shows that if you can argue from Beethoven forward, you can with equal justice argue to Æschylus backward.

Doubtful as I am that science will notably change either the nature or the task of art, though it may change expression, there are two powerful considerations that might alter my fideistic assumption. I am however, again troubled by vagueness of terms, since what I have in mind should be referred to the theory of science—to science as cosmic explanation rather than to science itself. We note, at least in the Western world, that when science powerfully touches the artistic imagination it often does so as cosmology. Thus not merely the notion of atoms appears in Lucretius' *De Rerum Natura;* what also appears in the poem, what makes it an epic of matter, is a theory of the universe which, if it places the gods far away from men, nevertheless gives them an intelligible abode and makes sense out of totality. So likewise the regularity of the Ptolemaic universe was accepted by art as plausible explanation, evident in the spheral harmony of mosaics at Ravenna, in Dante's *Divine Comedy,* and in Chaucer. The spatial and temporal enlargement of the universe of Copernicus and by and by that of Newton could be accommodated to the lay mind because it still represented order: the geometrical harmony of the Ptolemaic system was, so to say, merely supplanted by two other significant ideas—that of majesty, as in Milton's God and in God the Creator as depicted by William Blake; and a Euclidean relativity of size, as in Swift's Lilliputians and Brobdignagians and in Voltaire's Micromégas. Even when God ceased to be a celestial construction engineer and turned into a mighty central energy working in a teleological universe in the pre-Darwinian world, art could still appeal to a divine transcendental humanitarianism. In the Darwinian universe a linear conception of the survival of the fittest, whether as between individuals or as between species and societies, made direct sense. A statue like George Gray Barnard's *I Feel Two Natures Struggling Within Me,* a concept like the grotesque but powerful *Pillar of Life* by Vigelund at Oslo, the evolutionary eschatology of Wagner's *The Ring,* the Rougon-Macquart novels of Zola, the struggle of themes for mastery in Brahms' *Fourth Symphony* are expressions in varying ways in art of a theory of struggle seized on by the imagination. Indeed, the world-wide appeal of Herbert Spencer lay in the belief that his pretentious statement of a general theory of evolution was, precisely, a key to the riddle of the universe.

Now, only naïve persons think there is no order in the universe of Einstein, which is, on the contrary, a universe of abstract order. But lay persons have the right to think that there is in it no teleological order. The Einsteinian premises neither support nor destroy theology, as earlier cosmological assumptions did, they simply ignore theology. Theism and atheism are alike irrelevant to a world in which mass and energy are primary, not secondary, words. Such a universe, though it be one of the triumphs of the analytic mind, is neither human nor inhuman, humane nor inhumane, it simply *is.* Hence, the cosmic despair of the French existentialists. In such a universe all sorts of queer things can happen or seem to happen, such as the so-called twin effect, but though science fiction deals satisfactorily with this sort of phenomena, such a universe substantially sends man back where he came from—back, that is, to the Greeks or the Hindus. The Einsteinian universe is not a theater for either the drama of salvation or the drama of survival. It is not even a theater—though it may be an illusion, in which case the

Hindus will do. Or it may be merely a human construct, in which case the Greeks will do.

Much modernity, as in abstract painting, cerebral poetry, the curious sculptures of Henry Moore, atonal music and *musique concrète* confesses, in fact, the defeat of the old order, and in becoming art as experiment or art as discovery, gives up all pretense that art is ideal form. With that surrender it also abandons art as divine inspiration and art as a copy of eternal ideas. But is the change scientific or metaphysical?

It is conceivable that the Einsteinian universe is gradually altering the way art conceives time and space, although, before we too innocently regard this as an innovation, it is well to remember that multiple-place spaces simultaneously presented were an element in French medieval drama, that the simultaneous presentation of events occurring in temporal sequence was common alike in early Christian art and in Greek vase paintings, not to speak of the Egyptians, and that, just about the time Western artists had accepted the conventional perspective of Uccello as an absolute, we yearned to be Oriental or primitive and went in for new conventions. What seems more important is the shift in science from agrarian to urban values.

The beginnings of astronomy, geography, geometry, and other sciences were with shepherds in the Fertile Crescent, farmers in the Nile Valley, merchants in the cottage-economy of antiquity; or among the geomancy-minded agriculturists of ancient China. Modern science, though it builds telescopes on lonely mountain tops and establishes outposts in Antarctica, is the product of urban culture; that is, of university centers, research institutes, industrial plants, complex engineering facilities, electric power, and atomic energy produced not by farmers or coal-miners but by urban sophistication. Its priesthood is a city product, for whom basic education in rural school or village high school becomes less and less satisfactory and whose professional training is transferred to urban centers. Symbolical is the passing of the village doctor; symbolical also is the modern laboratory, virtually a fortress against disorderly nature outside. Communication, too, becomes urbanized. Contrast the articles in any specialized scientific journal with the leisurely correspondence of Darwin, whose backyard was his laboratory. The electron microscope replaces, as it were, the keenness of the human eye, and as we pry deeper into the secrets of matter we have to abandon the direct report of that crude instrument, the human ear.

Except in a few disciplines like geology this change has meant the displacement of wild nature as school and laboratory. The great race of naturalists dwindles—hence the nostalgia with which we read *Walden*—and some look happily forward to the abandonment of the crude outdoors as the sole source of our food supply. A kind of horror of wildness develops. Whereas Alexander Wilson, one of the founders of American ornithology, could make his way as a matter of course through the wilderness from Philadelphia to Niagara Falls on foot alone or with a single companion in 1804, our scientific expeditions take along a packaged urban culture—an internal combustion engine, drums of liquid fuel, a private electric plant, a portable drugstore, a radio, and of course scientific instruments skillfully tooled.

The horror of wildness contrasts sharply with the American attitude a hundred years ago. The difference appears in the arts. Advanced representational painting gives us city streets, not the Adirondacks or the Rockies, novels about the wilderness concern legendary mountain men or some historical figure like Daniel Boone, our music on like themes, such as Copland's *Appalachian Spring,* weaves archaisms into its texture, and bird-watching becomes the indulgence of the metropolitan few in Central Park or Mount Auburn Cemetery, and not as with Audubon or Catesby scientific discovery. Why not? From the city dweller who shall never know the quiet skies of Moses and Joshua the stars have been taken away by the same glow that curtails the effectiveness of the Mount Wilson observatory. Indeed, H. G. Wells' dream of whole cities under glass and Bulwer-Lytton's dream of whole races underground no longer seem fantastic. But into a city under glass as into a space-block skyscraper or into a city underground as into a septic basement man retreats, so to speak, as into an artificial beehive. All this alters the vocabulary of art, though it does not alter its age-old themes.

But is such a change a simple function of science in the world of the future? Or of technology? To say so is to oversimplify. Science both causes and results from cultural changes. True, our swarming cities avoid recurrent epidemics only by grace of sewage engineering and scientific prophylaxis, but, contrariwise, problems of the disposal of waste and the prevention of disease are created by a gregariousness that may not endure.

There was once a sophisticated city-culture in Crete, which we know because its arts proved more enduring than its scientific practices. Carl Sandburg, I am told, is no longer fashionable; nevertheless I conclude this commentary with a passage from his poem, "Four Preludes on Playthings of the Wind":

> The doors were cedar
> and the panels strips of gold

and the girls were golden girls
and the panels read and the girls chanted:
   We are the greatest city,
   the greatest nation:
   nothing like us ever was.
The doors are twisted on broken hinges.
Sheets of rain swish through on the wind
   where the golden girls ran and the panels
      read:
   We are the greatest city,
   the greatest nation:
   nothing like us ever was.

It has happened before.
Strong men put up a city and got
   a nation together,
And paid singers to sing and women
   to warble: We are the greatest city,
      the greatest nation:
      nothing like us ever was.
And while the singers sang
and the strong men listened
and paid the singers well
and felt good about it all,
   there were rats and lizards who listened
   . . . and the only listeners left now
   . . . are . . . the rats . . . and the lizards.*

Art knows it is well to be humble before even the triumphs of science.

* "Four Preludes on Playthings of the Wind" in *Smoke and Steel* by Carl Sandburg, copyright, 1920 by Harcourt, Brace & World, Inc.; copyright 1948, by Carl Sandburg. Reprinted by permission of the publisher.

A FAREWELL TO THE ENGLISH
DEPARTMENT

O N NOVEMBER FIFTEENTH, 1962, in Boston, a special counsel to the President of the United States addressed an audience of seven hundred at a meeting of the New England Council. I have no reason to think he was not correctly reported in the newspaper. The heart of his address was this sentence: "The chief business of New England has always been business." This seems to me one of the unfortunate statements of the year.

It reduces to no importance the struggle of seventeenth-century colonists to create at Plymouth, in Massachusetts Bay, at New Haven, at Hartford, in Rhode Island and Providence Plantations a new order of society under God. It overlooks the long conflict narrated by Francis Parkman between the Catholic French and the British Protestants, known to school children as Queen Anne's War, King George's War, and the French and Indian War. It passes over the effort after 1763 to mod-

This address was given at a banquet of the Department of English at Harvard University November 27, 1962, when I retired. It was later printed in the *Harvard Alumni Bulletin* and also as a pamphlet for private distribution. Copyright © 1963 by the Harvard Alumni Bulletin, Inc.

ernize the British empire, an effort that, failing, eventuated in the Declaration of Independence and the creation of the United States. It drains the glory from New England letters—Bryant, Emerson, Hawthorne, Melville, Longfellow, Harriet Beecher Stowe, and all the rest. It ignores the contributions by New England to education, beginning with the Boston Latin School in 1635 and continuing through the work of Horace Mann, Charles W. Eliot, James Bryant Conant, and the founders of scores of schools, academies, colleges, and universities in New England and out of it. It omits great names in general thought like those of Jonathan Edwards, Benjamin Silliman, John Adams, Charles S. Peirce, Willard Gibbs, Josiah Royce, George Santayana, and William James. It dismisses creation in the arts by geniuses such as Bulfinch, Richardson, Washington Allston, Winslow Homer, Charles Ives, and their kind. It ignores the enormous contributions of New England to law, medicine, technology, political science, theology, and science itself. But at any rate it parallels the statement by an earlier president, I regret to state from New England, that the business of the United States is business. To this still another New Englander (as he then was) properly retorted that the business of the United States is not business, it is civilization. I am quoting Felix Frankfurter.

It is not now fashionable to praise Daniel Webster, in part because he is supposed to have been unduly influenced by New England business. Nevertheless I shall quote him. One hundred and thirty-two years before the remark I cite, irked by some allegations about New England business—made by Senator Hayne of South Carolina—on the floor of that chamber, Daniel Webster said:

Mr. President, I shall enter no encomium upon Massachusetts. She needs none. There she is—behold her and judge for yourselves. There is her history; the world knows it by heart. The past, at least, is secure. There is Boston, and Concord, and Lexington, and Bunker Hill—and there they will remain forever. The bones of her sons, falling in the great struggle for independence, now lie mingled with the soil of every State from New England to Georgia; and there they will lie forever. And, sir, where American liberty raised its first voice; and where its youth was matured and sustained, there it still lives, in the strength of its manhood and full of its original spirit. If discord and disunion shall wound it—if party strife and blind ambition shall hawk at and tear it—if folly and madness—if uneasiness, under salutary and necessary restraint shall succeed to separate it from that Union, by which alone its existence is made sure, it will stand, in the end, by the side of the cradle in which its infancy was rocked; it will stretch forth its arm with whatever of vigor it may still retain, over the friends who gather round it; and it will fall, if fall it must, amidst the proudest monuments of its own glory, and on the very spot of its origin.

This is old-fashioned speaking. Many find it embarrassing. We no longer believe in rhetoric in any sense as one of the seven liberal arts, and we are incapable of Webster's diction, which seems to us Wagnerian and brassy. The appeal of his style has been killed by a number of things—television, radio, the microphone, newspaper prose, freshman English, and the assumption by departments of public speaking that the only way to make a successful public address is to pretend that you are not speaking in public. I am aware also that Webster may be tendentious. But I suggest he was at least addressing himself to the right tendency—a belief in historical culture.

Webster was steeped in the King James Bible. He knew Shakespeare and Milton almost by heart. He read Virgil and Cicero many times, regretted he had not studied Demosthenes more thoroughly, and talked over Latin literature with his friends. He read Locke, Jonathan Edwards, Blackstone, Burlamaqui, *Don Quixote,* the *Spectator* papers, Pope, Goldsmith, John Adams, Boswell, and many more. For its cadence and amplitude good judges have said his style resembles that of Burke, concerning whom Hazlitt remarked that if there were greater prose writers, they lay out of the course of his—Hazlitt's—study; and he surpassed Burke in his capacity to hold an audience. Who can forget Carlyle's description of Webster, "the tanned complexion, that amorphous crag-like face; the dull black eyes under their precipice of brows, like dull anthracite furnaces needing only to be blown; the mastiff mouth accurately closed—I have not traced so much of silent Bersirker-rage that I remember of in any man." I do not trace any Bersirker rage in the remark of the special counsel, but only a desire to please.

Behind Webster I find a long tradition of literature and eloquence. Behind the speech at the New England Council I find nothing except the possible existence of that shadow of a shade, the ghost writer. Possibly there is some connection between that version of New England history and some figures from the federal budget in 1961. In that year 71 percent of the expenditures for basic research went to the physical sciences, mathematics, and engineering; 26 percent to biology, medicine, and agriculture; 2 percent to the psychological sciences; 1 percent to the social sciences; and to the humanities nothing at all.

We have just escaped, or hope we have escaped, from

53

the dreadful danger of nuclear war. We like to feel that the freedom-loving nations have won at least a temporary respite and that the Communist nations have suffered a defeat. Whatever the eventual issue in Cuba proves to be, the general conflict has no foreseeable end. It is a battle for the spirit of man, not for men's stomachs nor for their pocketbooks, either of which could be easily filled, were there no antagonistic value systems in the world. What is likelier to hearten us in this contest—the naïve business ethos of 1962, which but confirms the Communists in their belief that materialism and profits are the principal concern of the United States, or Daniel Webster, with a whole tradition behind him, expressing, however imperfectly, a faith in the soul of a people?

The soul of a people, the past to which it looks back with pride and affection—these are not found in its IBM machinery or its tariff laws or its military might, but in its language, its literature, its philosophy, its religion, its art. "Give me," cried Andrew Fletcher of Saltoun, "the making of the songs of a nation, and I care not who makes its laws." This famous sentence, simple and profound, is known to everybody except politicians and practical men, who look upon human beings as bodies to be moved around, fed, cajoled, housed, and if necessary, shot at and buried.

Despite the statistics I have cited, I believe the future of the humanities to be immense. They stand now where Christian theology stood in the thousand-year contest with the Mohammedan world, which terminated with the siege of Vienna in 1683. If it took almost a thousand years to protect and establish the cultural unity of Western Europe, it will take at least that length of time to determine whether the culture of the West, the culture of the Slav, the culture of the Chinese, or some other culture is to conquer. At first sight the work of an English department seems to have nothing to do with this great issue. But if Western humanism, if the humanities in the United States, if the humanities at Harvard are weapons in this contest, scholars may not rest content with the analysis of process but must consider the presentation of ends.

Five dynamic systems of value struggle upon this planet—that of the Atlantic community, that of the Mohammedan world, that of the Slavs, that of Asia, and that of emergent Africa. Each of them has its own inner tensions. In the Atlantic community, for example, innumerable misunderstandings arise between the Ibero-American nations and ourselves. The alternations of strain and unity among the Mohammedan countries are matters of common knowledge. In the Slavic world the question of how far the Russia of Khrushchev continues and how far it denies a mystique of Russian destiny originating in Byzantium is a matter of enormous meaning to us. In Asia we have to reckon with the ancient cultures of India and China among others, each remarkably transformed from what it was, yet neither of them understandable without some knowledge of the timeless tradition in which it is embedded. What patterns are to take shape in Africa we cannot know, though we can hope that neither the segregationist madness at one end of that continent nor the unpredictable dictatorship of Nasser at the other will determine the outcome.

If the United States is not merely to survive but also make its way amid this immense confusion, it must begin by understanding itself. The nation now contains but will not face a cultural dilemma. The republic was built on certain philosophic principles evident in the writings of the founding fathers. These principles were common assumptions among progressive eighteenth-century thinkers, who studied Locke, Montesquieu, and the ancients, who accepted the faculty psychology of their time, and who assumed as a matter of course that man is sufficiently rational to choose his rulers wisely. Their vision was that of a happy agrarian republic.

By the generation of Emerson the basic interpretation of human nature was shifting from rationality to intuition, from geometry to dynamism, from mind to soul; and when one reads Emerson's attacks on State Street, together with those of Hawthorne, Melville, and others, one realizes that a split was developing—the split noted in the 1920's by Van Wyck Brooks when he said that one-half of America was descended from Benjamin Franklin the businessman and the other half from Jonathan Edwards the idealist.

But the soul disappeared in 1890 when, in his *Principles of Psychology,* William James banished it as a concept useless to the scientific psychologist. In the twentieth century the agrarian republic has also vanished into what Henry Miller calls our air-conditioned nightmare and what kindlier commentators describe as the triumph of our technological skills. There are other changes. One is the decline of the church as a guide of life. A second is the increasing importance of higher education as a surrogate for religion. A third is the disappearance of the radical left and the emergence of the radical right. A fourth is the uncritical acceptance of a shallow doctrine of human nature as fundamentally irrational. This theory is now the stock in trade of the arts and, unfortunately, of many humanists; and is flatly contradicted by the dazzling successes of rationality in other fields. Poets and novelists, filled with zeal for irrationalism, inconsistently continue to go to the dentist, the doctor, and the surgeon for physiological repair on scientific principles discovered by rational research.

The profound disharmony between the theory of human nature as inevitably irrational and of art as subliminal self-expression, and the triumphs of the intellect in a mensurational civilization is the principal cultural problem of our time. Doubtless, as René Dubos observes, civilizations commonly become intoxicated with their technological proficiency. But you do not correct the alleged inhumanity of a mensurational culture by celebrating the superiority of a non-rational art. No one desires to control the artist. But the humanist has the legitimate function of seeing the arts in terms of their general cultural responsibility and not merely in terms of themselves. Is not this the highest responsibility of scholarship? The duty of scholarship is to bring philosophy to the interpretation of the arts, not merely to derive its modes of interpretation from current practitioners of art and of criticism.

Whatever fashions may crowd the hour, the nobility of art and of scholarship must be that of the sculptor Ernst Barlach when he said: "What man can suffer and must suffer, the grandeur and the need of man: to that I am committed." The emphasis here is not on the easy way of suffering but on the difficult way of grandeur.

I hold therefore to the simple dogma that man is more than the sum of his historical mistakes. The weapons that threaten to destroy mankind are, it is true, the inventions of reason. They will not launch themselves but will be launched, if ever they are, by the ancient motives of fear, envy, or desire. Men do not starve or fight or die for the sheer pleasure of extinction but because they conceive their starving, fighting, or dying has something to do with values they believe in or are persuaded to accept. I

57

can understand the theater of the absurd, but I do not care to remain, a helpless spectator, in its auditorium. I think men are often irrational, but I think man is rational. Like other pessimists I require nobility; and I think history, if it be black with crime, treachery, and slaughter, is starred also with instances of heroism, beauty, and virtue. Not even contemporary criticism has hinted that Washington suffered from a power drive, Marcus Aurelius is an example of smothered envy, and Gautama Buddha the victim of a castration complex.

However professionally exciting it may be to hunt down water symbols in Poe, or Proust, or Pope, the humanist cannot forget that his primary responsibility is to the national culture, not to the Modern Language Association, and that oncoming generations, though they should be generously encouraged to believe that beauty is its own excuse for being, must also be strictly taught the changeless meaning of the three most powerful words in any dialect—justice, virtue, and love; concepts that arise out of history in spite of the fact that, or because, history too frequently denies them. The imperative task of humane teaching is, interpreting history, to lead men to ponder upon and accept the essentiality of these three words. For unless we are prepared to argue, as I am not, that the entire story of religion, philosophy, the arts, and the sciences moves in an illusory orbit that has nothing to do with justice, virtue, and love—unless we are egoists enough to believe that the whole horrible truth about the universe has been reserved for this unhappy generation to discover, we must as scholars steadily resist the easy implication that our fathers before us were the fools of illusion and that our only remaining duty is to impress upon the lineaments of history a blank and meaningless mask.

I cannot accept this facile solution to the problem at Harvard, the problem of the United States, or the problem of Western man. I think the duty of scholarship is to resist folly and expound wisdom wherever it can find the one and combat the other. It is but half a truth to assert that every age recreates the past in its own image. If this were so, all our knowledge would revolve like a whirligig every thirty years, and fixed points like Homer, Bach, Michelangelo, Immanuel Kant, and Shakespeare would not remain in any way stable. I believe that culture exists, that humane scholarship exists, not for the pleasure of a few professionals, the pleasures of technical analysis of style or symbol, text or score, but for larger humane and human ends. We have not achieved justice, virtue, and love on this planet, and perhaps we never shall, but to slacken in the search now, to abandon the age-long quest to followers of irrationality and fantastical theories—this is, indeed, the treason of the intellectuals. I see nothing naïve about fighting for a philosophy and expressing it as well as one can. Any other concept only plunges us into terror and darkness.

If ours were a business civilization only, it would in a few more years be one with the business civilizations of the Hittites and the Phoenicians. We have of course been taught all the way from the Greeks to Mr. Toynbee that cultures decay and vanish, and we have no reason to suppose that ours is eternal; but if we fall, as fall we must, we ought to seek to be remembered as guardians of the proudest monuments of Western art and philosophy and be recalled, if we are ever thought of, as among those who sought to do some work of noble note not unbecoming men that strove with gods.

SCHOLARSHIP AND THE
FUTURE TENSE

As I cannot consider humanistic scholarship a lonely or artificial activity, in order that we shall not misunderstand it or make wrong demands upon it I begin by noting certain parallels and differences between humanistic scholarship on the one hand, and the sciences and the social sciences on the other. I turn to science.

The aim of science differs from the aim of humanistic scholarship, in the first place, in that the ideal of science is to play down or banish the personal equation. We invent instruments that operate with a lesser and lesser degree of human interference. We carry on scientific inquiry not subjectively but in public time and space. The essence of experimentation is that whatever A does can be repeated in like circumstances by B, C, D, and E; and when this is done we accept the results, if uniform, as a

Under the title "Development in Humanistic Scholarship" this paper was originally part of a symposium on the future of learning in this country and abroad. The symposium celebrated the seventy-fifth anniversary of the Graduate School of the University of Pennsylvania, and the papers delivered were printed under the editorship of Charles E. Bowe and Roy F. Nichols at the University of Pennsylvania Press in 1960.

statement of or approximation to general truth.

In the humanities, however, the personal equation plays a continuing rôle. The study of a great cultural period—for example, the Renaissance—takes into account and, indeed, rests upon the interpretations of scholars like Burkhardt, Symonds, and Bernard Berenson, not merely because of deference paid to authority but because the very data under inspection are, as it were, the creations of the judgment of scholars. It is true that works of art must please many and please long, but it is true also that masterpieces are created by opinion, that they serve as centers for collecting data concerning them, their predecessors, their rivals, their imitators, and in the long run this kind of information generates our notions of culture in a given period.

Science is, in the second place, an activity principally in the present tense. It surrenders its own past to the humanities as part of history. The past is for the scientist a series of guesses at truth, and the enterprise of science is to refine the lucky hits and destroy the unlucky. Thus the theory that a universal ether permeates all things is now an erroneous hypothesis that has for science only curiosity value. To the cultural historian, however, this theory may be a fundamental datum. Great classes of scientific problems, to be sure, involve lapse of time; yet it is in general true that science lives in the present and looks to the future.

Scholarship, however, tends to look backward. Humane learning does not ignore the living thinker, present art, or current developments in fields like semantics, theology, or theories of value, but the main staple of scholarship is the past. Indeed, only because this is true do we know anything reliable about history, and on this knowledge library, museum, and university depend. The masterpiece of tradition, the great thinker known by his influence, the cultural era to which we look back with desire—these are principal concerns of the scholar.

In the third place, a large part of practical scientific enterprise is involved with predictive judgments. We want to know that the bridge will sustain its traffic, the building be safe, the chemistry of the dye invariable, the drug secure and relevant to the disease. We likewise desire to predict within statistical probability the chances of death or the percentage of recoveries from a given operation, and we shape policy by these predictions, which are predictions of utility. Non-utilitarian predictions, like the setting of a date for the return of a comet, also give us a strong feeling of intellectual peace, so much so that we accept a phrase like "scientific control" as natural and seemly, and are shocked by a term like "theological control." But theological control made excellent sense in the year 1000.

Humanistic scholarship is on the whole incapable of trustworthy predictive judgments. In the first place, the principal concern of scholarship is, as I have said, with the past. In the second place, the humanist is helpless to prophesy the appearance of genius, and yet genius produces much of what he studies. In the third place, even though there is an admitted vague law of action and reaction in the history of culture, we cannot know in any present period what the opposing movement is going to be, since reaction may take any one of a number of possible forms. For example: in 1908 the hope of American music lay with the romantic rhetoric of Edward MacDowell, who died that year. No musicologist could —at least no musicologist did—predict that in 1909 the unknown Charles Ives was to begin composing his "Concord Sonata," a piece of piano music revolutionary in its effect. This is, if you will, a prediction of taste, but predictions of scholarship are equally at the mercy of accident, genius, guesswork, and the side-effects of something else. Accidents enable us to decipher the Rosetta Stone, discover the Sumerians, uncover temples in Yucatan, and learn about Greek life in the third century B.C. through the chance preservation of the mimes of Herondas in a papyrus from Fayoum. Looking back, the scholar can discover orderly development in time; looking forward, his guess is no better than yours or mine. If these considerations be valid, as I think they are, it is useless for administrators to expect from humanists the kind of program of development they are used to in fields like physics, medicine, or geology.

In so far as he seeks the genetic explanation of social phenomena or adopts the historical point of view, the social scientist, particularly the anthropologist and anyone who strives like Pareto or Marx to shape a general theory, is committed to the temporal process and suffers from the same inability to prophesy as does the humanist. Extrapolation is a tool of limited use; and painful contrasts between what the world became and what it was expected to become are commonplaces in history. Nevertheless, we expect from the social sciences empirical predictions of great value. Our industrial economy, our social policies, and in some degree, at least, our political actions depend upon expert prophecy. The wide acceptance of planning in the twentieth century, however distasteful any particular plan may be, is a function of this confidence. Judgments take such shape as: "We may expect the population of the United States in 1988 to be of such-and-such magnitude"; and if this prediction differs *toto caelo* from the prediction "Halley's comet will return in 1985," it is nonetheless enormously useful. The predictions are of course subject to the interruptions of catastrophe, whether natural as in the case of an earthquake, or man-made as in the case of war.

Despite their utility, we must, however, distinguish. We do within a certain tolerance of error fix insurance rates and plan highway systems. But we are less certain about long-range prophecy. Consider the current doctrine that social adjustment is a mark of a well-rounded personality, a theory that has had radical effects upon our schools, the managerial function, American fiction, and our attitude towards marriage. Who can say what the long-range result upon American society is going to be? We note historic revolutions in value judgments concerning slavery, women, laziness, and the control of government by a priesthood; but we cannot surely know whether a particular component of our culture makes for another historic revolution of like kind.

In so far as the social sciences aspire to the condition of science, they seek to discover general habits, principles, modes, averages, means, or laws of behavior, with the purpose of diminishing the area of the unknown and increasing our knowledge of the motives and actions of men. Theoretically, knowledge is an end in itself; practically, however, advances towards general principles mean advances towards modes of control. It would be absurd to say that the social scientist desires to control our behavior. Nevertheless the feeling of uneasiness evident in books like *Brave New World, 1984,* and *Fahrenheit 451* indicates genuine fear of the misuse of the results of research in social science, particularly in social psychology, nor is this fear confined to imaginative writers, for it helps to shape works like *The Organization Man, The Power Elite,* and others. The social scientist may retort that the potential misuse of knowledge is no reason for cutting off the pursuit of knowledge; and if the ideal of research in all fields were pure Aristotelian contemplation, his retort would be crushing. But the uses to which knowledge is put are part of the very data of social science; and in a culture of which television, radio, and advertising are components of that social pattern wherein research is done, it may be that the governing ideals we work for are to be discovered in other areas of experience and not in social science and in science alone. *Quis custodiet custodes?* When, to take a simple instance, institutions of higher learning seriously offer courses in advertising psychology—that is, expert instruction in ways to smother judgment and induce impulse-buying—one realizes with a shock that the expertise in such instruction depends upon the scholarship of men as remote from the course as Bagehot, Tarde, Trotter, and Gustave Le Bon. No social scientist worth his salt is in the least interested in the manipulation of research for shallow ends, and I am indicting neither social science nor the university; I am merely pointing to the cultural condition that led the late Edward Sapir to contrast the telephone girl lending her capacities to the manipulation of a technical routine of high efficiency value and no spiritual nutriment, with the American Indian inefficiently spearing salmon but far freer of the sense of spiritual frustration that haunts our age, despite the brilliant work of scientists and social scientists.

Now it is in no sense the fault of social science if mankind is suspicious of regularity and pattern. The fact that one can predict with security that x thousands of Americans in my age bracket will die in 1960 does not mean that I am going to die in 1960. The hypothesis that the American power elite succeed, but succeed only within what their historian calls "the American system of organized irresponsibility" does not negate the worth of responsibility. Perhaps one of the most cogent comments upon the social sciences is Josiah Royce's great essay on "Self-Consciousness, Social Consciousness, and Nature." In vain does scholarship establish the most admirable patterns of identity and difference, in vain do we reduce social behavior to graph and curve, in vain do we talk about the relativity of value judgments and moral systems. I remain I, unique egotist, from the dawning to the dimming out of consciousness. It is upon this profound, and if you like subliminal truth, that humane learning is built. But humane learning immediately develops a paradox. Its purpose is to sustain and enrich the individual, but in order to do so it concerns itself with a mystical general concept called Man. By Man it means neither the complex aggregations we know as nations, societies, tribes, or clans; nor yet the equally complex integer, prisoner of time, space, and gravity; product of biology, physical chemistry, and inherited instincts; and former of habits, known to science as *Homo sapiens,* to medicine as a patient, and to social science as a sibling, a voter, a customer, or a captive of tabu. By Man humane learning means man's best image of himself.

That the claim of humane learning has general validity can be inferred by a curious observation. The humanistic scholar is not perturbed if somebody says he is not a scientist, not a social scientist. He may, indeed, retort that he has turned linguistics into a science and that as art historian, bibliographer, or archaeologist, he gladly uses tools and devices science puts into his hand, just as he may note developments in economics, sociology, political science, and anthropology to which he contributes and which contribute to him. But during the many years I have been concerned with the theory and practice of humanistic scholarship I have never known scientists or social scientists who failed to wince if somebody stated or inferred they were not humane savants pursuing humane ends. They were right to protest. Their sensitivity is no proof, however, of an innate superiority in humanists or of their depravity; it is evidence that intelligent men desire out of life something more than intellectual efficiency.

The subject of humane learning is the distillation of human experience in time. The English vocabulary it uses includes terms like excellence, beauty, resignation, courtesy, wisdom, courage, duty, and insight rather than terms like know-how, elite, control, behavior pattern, exogamy, managerial, worthy leisure-time activity, and training for leadership. In other languages humane learning dares to use words like *esprit* and *Geist;* and if I were to choose from my limited knowledge a single noun that most nearly expresses its philosophical aim, I think I would go to the Latin and select *pietas,* meaning reverence for life, for tradition, for individual honor, and for such hints at divinity as are vouchsafed imperfect man. These are individualized, not social, not scientific concepts.

The purpose of humane learning is normative, not absolute; it accepts moral relativity without denying morality, just as it accepts comparisons in art and philosophy without therefore inferring that art and philosophy are mere social phenomena; and, in no sense hostile to contemporary achievement, it reminds living men not to confuse the state of art and thought in their own era with the total purpose of human experience. It offers, in sum, not a program nor a prediction, but a point of view, a philosophy broader than systems of philosophy, an insistence that wisdom is more than knowledge. For, at the

67

ending end of science and of social science, the unanswered question is still: Why should we be trying to do what we try to do? Humane learning, essentially conservative, exists to remind Man that he is neither a mere animal nor a mere physical and psychological tropism, but a unique sensibility capable of what the Germans call Becoming, an individualized personality that may in time achieve moral character.

If such be the ideal, what are our present pressing problems in reaching it? I omit all questions of the financial support of the humanities, wretched though that support presently is in comparison with our total national wealth; and insist that our culture faces at least two crucial issues, one internal and one external. The internal one is this: The humanities were once defined as polite learning, were once, in other words, the possession of an elite. How, for our classless society, shall we translate a tradition of aristocratic sensibility into popular terms? How shall we both offer exclusiveness to the masses and persuade them to accept it? This is a grave pedagogical problem we have not solved, which we are trying to solve sentimentally, and which is going to plague us for many years. The external problem is this: How, in a world situation in which our policy makers have on the whole failed to check the growth of communism, can scholarship, democracy being on the defensive, help us to sustain a vigorous and affirmative culture? Our present resources are clearly not enough. In the words of Dr. Robert R. Wilson: "Assuming that civilization survives the invention of this ultimate weapon [the hydrogen bomb], the human spirit will be challenged often and perhaps even more seriously by future developments in science and technology. For me the question is: Are scientists to attain the heightened sense of moral values which will enable them to determine the direction of these developments with humanistic and humanitarian ends in view, or will humanists and humanitarians attain an understanding of scientific values that will allow them to determine the wise direction of science? I suspect that civilization will best be served by a true fusion—at least a close mutual understanding—of science, the humanities and politics." *

I agree. Therefore the first task of graduate work in the humanities is to raise, not lower, the intellectual water-table from its present adolescent plane to something like maturity. Some three or more decades ago John Livingston Lowes, then president of the Modern Language Association, said in his annual address that in his observation the best men go into science, the second best into the social sciences, and the third-raters into the humanities. There are exceptions to all rules, but I have seen little since Mr. Lowes spoke that leads me seriously to alter his judgment. If any of you has been recently involved in making a distinguished appointment in some branch of the humanities, you will, I think, sadly agree. We cannot advance mature scholarship in this country so long as we are content with amiable persons taking mediocre degrees that meanly fulfill minimum requirements. I, for one, am flatly opposed to current emotional drives to make the degree easier and shorter. Knowledge multiplies in all fields; the humanist is under greater pressure to deal with rich, exotic cultures; and I cannot for the life of me see how you increase depth and cultural range by decreasing the depth and range of a training program.

In the second place, I am of opinion that we must

* Review of *Brighter than a Thousand Suns,* by Robert Jungk, *Scientific American,* CXCIX (December 1958), 149.

demand a far more mature command of languages (including our own) than we are now getting. The decline and fall of foreign language requirements for the Ph.D. is understandable. At the opening of the century the old-line philologist, still wedded to a nineteenth-century evolutionary concept, reduced the Ph.D. in departments of literature to a philological pattern. Both the direct and the side-effects were disastrous. The teaching of foreign languages declined; departments other than literary ones found the requirements an impediment, not a help; and the pendulum has swung so far in the other direction that most candidates in literature have now no real command of linguistic science and most Ph.D.'s no real control of any foreign language whatsoever. The present program of the Modern Language Association, by insisting that a foreign language must be begun in childhood, does something; and there are those who are cheered by current federal legislation favoring foreign languages as essential to national defense. I, too, am grateful. But a philosophy promoting linguistic study on the mere ground of utility does nothing for cultural insight. We need something richer than a minimum ability to interrogate a prisoner of war or inquire about iron and steel. Language is par excellence the instrument of humanistic scholarship. I submit that most Americans are innocent of the central meaning of this truth. Our scandalous lack of control over languages is the more serious because we need to know more rather than fewer languages, and to know them better. If the Chinese, the Russians, the Indians, and other ancient Asian and African peoples can learn English, it is surely not beyond the capacity of young America to learn at least one foreign language thoroughly and well. The disservice wrought by the simple-minded belief that everything has been, or can be, translated is very great, especially in a period when we are trying to penetrate into the psychology of cultures remote from our own.

In the third place, we must consider whether our present pattern for the Ph.D. degree is the only possible pattern. Inherited from nineteenth-century geneticism, that pattern is vertical, not horizontal; that is, most departments of the humanities expect the student to know the whole field in historical order before he specializes in any part of it. There is much to be said for this doctrine, especially in relatively unfamiliar cultural areas. But our departmentalization plays us false when the problem concerns a great, familiar cultural epoch. Take romanticism. In theory the musicologist interested in romantic music is required to get up a total knowledge of musical history before he gets around to, say, Schumann; a scholar interested in Schelling must master the historical aspects of philosophy before he travels to the Jena of 1798; and similar are the cases of the student of poetry, linguistic theory, theology, painting, architecture, the history of ideas, or for that matter history itself. As a result, romanticism gets departmentalized out of existence. I constantly meet students of the eighteenth century without any musical knowledge; students of Horace with no slightest trace of interest in architecture; specialists in Renaissance poetry ignorant of Renaissance painting; Ph.D.'s in the Victorian novel who have never heard of the names of Eastlake, Frith, Pugin, Robert Stephenson, Maclise, Paxton, and other shapers of Victorian culture. The consequence is a lack of engagement between the specialist and a total cultural interpretation. Surely specialization can exist horizontally as well as vertically. I do not see that getting up sympathetic knowledge of eighteenth-century music, eighteenth-century painting, eighteenth-century

71

philosophy, and eighteenth-century taste is any greater burden upon a student of eighteenth-century prose than getting up the total history of the English language and of English literature before he gets to the eighteenth century. I do not see that an incompatibility of taste with respect to music on the part of the philosophical specialist is any greater obstacle to a mature and flexible interpretation of learning than the incompatibility between, say, an interest in Schopenhauer and the requirement that the scholar shall be equally well grounded in Plato, Aristotle, medieval scholasticism, logical positivism, and the optimism of Leibnitz before he gets around to the *World as Will and Idea*. If we were to set up mature training programs in great cultural periods that would include the essential interests of these periods, we would do on a mature level what we are already fumbling after in our undergraduate courses in general education. I think we shall always have graduate programs shaped to historical perspective; surely, however, this does not mean we cannot also shape programs directed towards the interpretation in unified order of those great cultural epochs that have molded human destiny. We accept the Ph.D. in English language and literature: special field, romantic literature. Is this so changeless a concept that we cannot think of a Ph.D. in medieval culture: special field, Latin lyric poetry?

I shall rest content with these three suggestions. It seems unnecessary to point out that with the passing of the European age, the history, the art, the moral systems and the philosophy of Islam, the Slavic world, and the vast and varied populations of Asia and Africa require us, without abandoning Greece, Rome, and the Atlantic community, to increase vastly the number of young humanists competent to work appreciatively in what used to be thought of as merely exotic material. We cannot indefinitely regard the new nations emerging in Africa as mere objects of missionary zeal or of anthropological inquiry only. I shall say nothing about what I feel to be the greatest need of humanistic scholarship in certain fields, including the modern one; namely, a knowledge of the theory and philosophy of science (something that must not be confused with an ability to understand scientific articles); and equally in certain fields, a comprehension, not of technical articles in the social sciences but of the cultural implications of forms of social theory. I shall likewise pass over another problem that would take long to discuss—that raised by the president of the American Historical Association in 1957 when he advised scholars to master certain forms of psychology and psychological theory, an idea of first moment in the interpretation of all the arts. I have likewise said nothing about possible new fields of learning, for, as I indicated earlier, I think predictive judgments in humanistic scholarship are almost impossible to make. Finally, I am convinced that it is sheer folly to talk about the Ph.D. in the humanities as an obstacle to teaching, or to assume that we are somehow going to study and enrich American culture by a mere teaching degree. The concept of the scholar-teacher seems to me central and unshakable. I cannot conceive of teaching without scholarship, though I have seen it tried; and I cannot conceive of scholarship that does not give out or give forth or, if you will, simply give—and that, on any mature level, is teaching. What I would most deeply and persistently urge is that scholarship is a public duty, not a private delight; that if it is the duty of the state—by which I mean *res publica* in general—to support humane learning, it is the reciprocal duty of humane learning to support the state, by which I mean the Great Society

73

Josiah Royce dreamed about, not the evasive here and now of the noisy politician. The prospects before humane learning are the most exciting in my lifetime. Can the graduate schools and the learned societies rise to the great occasion? With the hope that they can and will, I conclude my case.

THE
HUMANITIES
IN
EDUCATION

THE USES OF THE PAST

I N THESE REMARKS I propose to discuss first, the haziness of the term, general education; second, general education as a surrogate for liberal education; third, some of the difficulties in teaching general education, more particularly in the humanities as a whole and then, specifically, in the types of historical instruction, both literary and cultural, that have developed. I shall conclude with the daring suggestion that we shall teach more if we teach less.

I face several difficulties in delivering this minority report of one, or, if that phrase be too noble, now raising my barbaric yawp over the roofs of the school houses, or if that be too literary, uttering my solitary squawk of protest against sweeping generalities and prodigious claims. After a good many years of teaching courses in general education and some years of reading about it, I feel like Bertrand Russell, who once said of his specialty: "In higher mathematics we do not know what we are

Under the title "The Uses of the Past in General Education" this paper was delivered at a meeting of the Advanced Administrative Institute in July, 1965, and published in the *Harvard Educational Review* in the Winter number, 1966.

doing and we do not know why we are doing it." General education has been construed to mean education for everybody, an interpretation that would make it tantamount to universal education, however that term has been defined; it has been talked about as corrective education—that is, general education is a kind of straightening device employed to cure the bends of too much vocational or specialized education; it has been used to signify what we once called adult education and it has been loosely employed to mean an acquaintance, usually superficial, with the sciences, the humanities, the social sciences, and the arts, provided that you do not stay long enough with any one of these branches of learning to learn very much about it. If you stay long enough to learn something thoroughly about one of these great branches of knowledge, or, more particularly, some subdivision of these great branches, you are likely to turn into a physicist, a literary critic, or a social worker. By sticking with general education, however, the theory is that you will avoid what is known as narrow specialism, or will at least correct that specialism by acquiring a broad background. It occurs to almost nobody, at least in the discussions I have listened to, that what is narrow may also be deep and that what is broad may also be shallow.

In order to avoid the charge of being merely peevish, let me say at once that the aim of the theory of general education was and is generous, whether in the secondary schools or in the colleges. Not to know the names of Leonardo da Vinci and Beethoven, not to have read *Hamlet* or *Crime and Punishment,* not to know the second law of thermodynamics or the truth that the carrying power of a stream varies as the eighth power of the velocity, not to know that Lee surrendered at Appomattox and that Herodotus was the father of history—gaps like these, it was held, meant that you were not a fully educated person. On the other hand, the spirit of mischief leads me mildly to inquire why an acquaintance with great historical names requires the instructional staff to ignore or undervalue an acquaintance with science fiction, the splendid form that the novel has taken in our time, the extraordinary progress made in astrophysics during the twentieth century, and the economic philosophy which, abandoning most monetary theory up to now, has led virtually all nations of the world to substitute fiat money for gold and silver—surely as astonishing a revolution as that we associate with a name like Einstein. But as I do not wish to get into another argument over the two cultures of Lord Snow, let me return to my muttons.

I assume that general education came in, particularly in the colleges but immediately thereafter in the high schools, because it was felt that the old concept of liberal education had broken down. Up to World War I or thereabout, the American high school still retained some vestigial remnants of the impress that the late nineteenth century had put upon it. One of its important functions was that of being a college preparatory school; courses in stenography and typewriting were still below the educational salt. It was a school that likewise bore the impress of a middle-class, white, Anglo-Saxon, Protestant culture, and therefore its graduates had, in some mild degree, a common core of values on which the college could operate. High-school courses had not yet proliferated. The high-school population was still small enough to be manageable. Parents were not yet afraid of their children, and the police had not yet trained German shepherd dogs to help them control teen-age riots. Since that happier era the high-school population has enormously increased in size and in heterogeneity of race, creed, and culture, thinking about the high school has more and more tended to run in megalopolitan terms, and an important and troubling element in the high-school situation has been not merely vandalism but unemployment. But these familiar considerations require no discussion from me.

General education in the colleges and in the high schools, which have perhaps played the sedulous ape to the universities too often for their own good, was, I take it, intended to replace, even if artificially, the common cultural core that had disappeared. I may note, incidentally, that I am aware of the movement to improve high-school science teaching, the teaching of foreign languages in the public schools, and the drive to do something about high-school instruction in general. All these are, in a sense, drives in the direction of better specialized teaching, and they do not (except indirectly) affect the sense of need that induced our enthusiasm for general education.

General education differs importantly, I suggest, from the older concept of liberal education, though the two ideas have some elements in common. The older concept of liberal education sprang from the purpose of the liberal arts as inherited from the Middle Ages, modified by the Renaissance, and transmitted to the American Republic. It was based upon some knowledge of the ancient world, including some knowledge of Latin, since Greek proved too difficult for the grandchildren of grandfathers who had studied Greek; and its original aim was the making of a gentleman or a gentlewoman according to the precepts of Castiglione and Matthew Arnold. In this century the rigors of liberal education softened from gentlemanliness to the genteel; and genteel values were essentially middle-class values, which, paradoxically, became more and more meaningless as more and more American families approached the condition of being middle-class. Books were central in liberal education, and science was admitted because it had been originally known as natural philosophy and was therefore not technical but philosophical.

A second important component of the older American concept of liberal education was that during the nineteenth century, particularly in its last half, the explanation of things including the art of literature, was sought in their origins. A generic explanation was supposed to be a true explanation. The ways by which any institution or tradition came into being whether it was the New England town meeting or the five-act play, were supposed to be sufficient explanation of the use and goodness of, to continue with my examples, the five-act play and the town meeting. Hence the one-volume histories of English or American literature that used to be taught in the high schools; hence the doctrine that the Pilgrim and the Puritans, following an ancient Germanic instinct for liberty, came here in search of political and religious freedom. The explanation, at least in the high schools, did not apply to all the arts and sciences; music and drawing, for example, were learned absolutely and not historically, and though civics classes cast a backward glance at the origins of the American Constitution and the constitutions of the several states, science did not. The elements of physics or chemistry or botany were, like the elements of music, absolutes to be learned. So was mathematics. So was Latin grammar. Despite these great exceptions the concept of a liberal education in this older period was colored by genetic explanation.

It would be tedious to relate the ways by which the-

81

ories of general education as a substitute for liberal education and a surrogate for culture in an apartment-house civilization came into being. Columbia, I think, led the way; Harvard got out its famous and influential report; and the high schools, at a genuine loss for some governing curricular idea, took on at least some portion of the concept of general education. As established, general education commonly fell into three grand divisions: courses in science for the nonscientific, courses in the social sciences, and courses in the humanities. The great subject of history nobody ever quite knew what to do with. If it was a social science, it belonged in that bracket; if it was an art, it belonged with the humanities. I shall treat it as one of the humanities—as, indeed, a central part of the humanities.

New brooms sweep clean; and the original teachers of courses in general education were enthusiastic, whether courses swept over the world in two years as did some of the Columbia courses, or were split into beginning and advanced courses as at Harvard, or, as in some high schools, turned into rapid surveys of world history or glimpses in succession at boat-building among the Egyptians, the education of a Roman boy, moats and castles in medieval England, a reconstruction of the Globe Theater, and a reading of excerpts from Benét's *John Brown's Body*. But by and by difficulties appeared. Topflight scientists, who seemed to regard general education courses in science as either propaganda or a defense mechanism, preferred in these exciting days to return to their laboratories and their research—otherwise they would fall behind in the procession. The social scientists were less involved but still there were those government jobs and, moreover, a kind of haziness hung over the concept of general education courses in social science. The humanists, by and large, hung on because they were mainly doing in an altered context what many of them had been doing before. Nevertheless, they also ran into certain great difficulties. Neither their own linguistic competence nor that of their students permitted them to read some great texts in the original tongues, so that perforce they had to resort to translation; and though the art of translation has notably improved in the last thirty or forty years, it was always the same texts that were being translated. Conferences were held, studies of the theory and practice of general education were subsidized, a magazine or two was published, books were got out. The goal was noble; but how reach the goal?

Here and there courses in general science "worked," but the alteration in science courses wrought as the result of pressures from the National Science Foundation, the National Defense Education Act, the books of James Bryant Conant, and other forces led a good many persons to the position that it was better to teach one science well and philosophically than to teach a potpourri of all the sciences badly. An example of this shift in attitude is found at the new University of California, San Diego at La Jolla, where the staff has concluded that the best way to acquaint even a non-scientific student with the nature and method of science is to teach him one science well. I am less familiar with changes in the social sciences, though in so far as general education courses in the social sciences are presumed to prepare the student for living in what we quaintly call today's world, I am under the impression that anthropology and social psychology are up and economics and political science are, relatively speaking, down. This shift, if it has occurred—and I am not certain of it except in one or two colleges—has meant, I take it, that the best way to shock the student into some comprehension of a complex technological culture may be to present him with a simpler culture and with elemental psychological truths. If this be the idea, it requires an enormous and difficult shift in pedagogical emphasis and attitude, one that I may call de-education and re-education. By de-education I mean the ability to get outside one's own cultural pattern, and by re-education I mean cultivating the capacity to accept some simpler culture at its face value, not to look down on it. I think the attraction of the Peace Corps to some youngsters and the wide vogue of folk singing among the rising generation may be indications that such a shift is possible. But it throws an enormous burden on the teacher.

I shall, however, confine myself to the humanities and particularly to history, subjects I am supposed to know a little something about. The humanities are (or is?) a loose term, the exact meaning of which no two persons agree upon. In the national foundations, for example, there is a prevalent fallacy that confuses the humanities with the creative arts, and a general tendency to play down scholarship and play up creativity. Both are good things in themselves; but I submit that supporting the arts is not the same thing as supporting the humanities and that the more we plug for the contemporary artist and neglect historical development, the more we induce the feeling that the past was only an imperfect anticipation of the present, and that the then is the same as the now. I shall return to this problem in a moment.

Two central components of general education in the humanities constantly recur. The first is that general education in the humanities has something to do with the history of ideas. That the humanities have a great deal to do with the history of ideas is patent, but my random observation of the history of ideas as taught in these

84

courses is that this history is somewhat oddly conceived. It is mostly the history of what I may call literary ideas. By literary ideas, I mean ideas that are confined principally to books. The line of development of scientific theories and scientific ideas; the ways by which modern Americans have come to a code of ethics in sports, any violation of which instantly makes the headlines; a history of invention; a history of engineering; a history of legal ideas or of technology or of medicine or of religious ideas—these notions are somewhat badly served in our present instruction. So far as that goes, some philosophy of the relation of the sexes, which would seem to be of some consequence, since we are supposed to be undergoing a sexual revolution of some sort, would seem relevant if difficult. As, however, I am of the opinion that the characteristic weakness of our instruction in general education is that we try to cover too much territory and therefore cover it hurriedly and badly, I am not urging that present or future courses be extended or expanded to include even these important components of our industrial and megalopolitan culture; I merely note that when one speaks of the history of ideas as an element in general education, one speaks of it in a somewhat Pickwickian sense.

A second component is great books. These volumes, masterpieces of the past, are studied for the light they can throw on our troubled times. They are expected to help us live in the age of the hydrogen bomb; and I suppose they do, in some degree, aid us, though a visitor from Mars, listening to our radio, looking at our television, and reading our newspapers and weekly magazines, might conceivably ask precisely how they aid us, what impression they make on pupils or students, and whether courses in great books have essentially altered American business life, political life, foreign policy, or the quality of our church services, or our notions of housing, or our concept of the family and the home. These queries may, of course, be premature; yet we have been teaching Shakespeare for a great many decades, and it does seem fair to ask how far the quality of Broadway shows has been influenced for the better by the required reading of *Hamlet*.

But this is not the real puzzle. Great books have, most of them, been with us much longer than contemporary life has been with us. The values we read into them may not be their lasting values. It may just be true that we somewhat falsify great books (and in due proportion great music and great art and great architecture and great systems of philosophy and of theology) by assuming that they were written with us in mind. It may be, if I may use an old-fashioned phrase, that they were written with eternity in mind, or, to be a little more realistic, that they were written for an immediate need and an immediate audience that had no notion of us in their minds. It is easy to twist the original occasion of a book into a coarse facsimile of our own problems. We should not so much use contemporary problems to illuminate great books as use great books to illuminate the age in which they first appeared and also those elements in human existence that do not greatly vary from the days of Job to the days of Lyndon Johnson. We suffer, it is said, from something called *Angst;* we suffer, or at least the young among us are said to suffer, from something called an identity crisis. Job also suffered from *Angst,* but his woe was not what we mean by the word; and I find it difficult to see in what sense a sound knowledge of *Paradise Lost* is going to solve anybody's identity crisis, whatever the stormier periods of John Milton's domestic life may have been. It

86

is one thing to interpret a work of art, and another to twist it. If we were all really Christians, for example, Bunyan's *Pilgrim's Progress* might once more be studied as it was studied by Meg, Jo, Beth, and Amy in *Little Women*. Not being Christians, we prefer Kierkegaard and Jonathan Swift. In other words, the modern moralizing of older texts does not seem to me to differ essentially from earlier moralizing of older texts except that we moralize from philosophical foundations that are shaky and not from religious belief.

I have two other observations to make on the great books enthusiasm. If the purpose of reading these books is either to make us understand how other people lived in past time or to aid us to live in present time, why great books? Why not some little ones? Quite as much light is thrown upon nineteenth-century living by Mrs. Gaskell's simple and charming novel, *Cranford,* as is thrown by Tolstoy's enormous *War and Peace,* admittedly a greater book. The life pictured in *Cranford* is that of a village culture quite as alien as that in *War and Peace* and therefore quite as striking. Moreover, *Cranford* is written in limpid English and is not a translation. I do not wish to throw out all the great books, but I would like to subdue the habit they have of crowding into lecture hall and class room and squeezing out all the little books. Dante's *Divine Comedy* is masterly, but nobody would suspect from reading it that anybody in the Middle Ages ever laughed or had a jolly time; and I suggest that the rather appalling ruggedness of Dante could be softened if we led students into reading that most charming of medieval love stories, *Aucassin and Nicolette,* or listening to a record of Carl Orff's picturesque setting of the *Carmina Burana.* This hints, at least, that there were sexy undergraduates as early as the century of Dante's birth.

87

My second difficulty with the great books is that I cannot discover on what principle, if any, they have been chosen. There is a curious imitativeness in all the lists I have seen. It is as if these were all drawn up by members of some academy—perhaps, in Wallace Stevens's phrase, an Academy of Fine Ideas—but I have an unhappy feeling that convention and a fear of not being in the fashion influence these lists more than does the conviction that the library might vary from time to time and from place to place. I have no objection to Fine Ideas; I merely think there are other sorts of interesting notions. Plato is always there, usually Plato's *Republic,* that apology for an elitist state, taught with great earnestness to students who are struggling to make democracy work in Selma, Alabama. I seldom, however, find the *Meditations* of Marcus Aurelius Antoninus in these lists, though the great Stoic emperor seems to me, at least, to bear more directly upon eternal problems of courage and endurance. St. Augustine's *Confessions* is there, too—a great book of course—but seldom the confessions of earthier and less saintly sinners like the *Autobiography of Benvenuto Cellini. The Divine Comedy,* or parts of it, usually gets taught; Goethe's *Faust,* or parts of it, usually does not, albeit Spengler, in *The Decline of the West,* said the Faustian spirit is the spirit of modernity. We apply ourselves diligently to Sophocles's *Oedipus Tyrannus;* we omit, or tend to omit, Sheridan's *The Rivals,* apparently because we think Sheridan's joyous farce might add to the popularity of *Mad* magazine. If this explanation be untenable, I have no other guess as to why laughter is at a discount in these programs—except, of course, that education is an extremely serious affair, as any manager of educational television will inform you as he tries to lure you into his studio.

In general education, the humanities have become the usual instrument for keeping the past meaningful to all students; that is, the future scientist and the future social scientist are not expected to take any other courses that deal with the past. The thesis I am propounding with reference both to history in these courses and to the great books idea—and I ought to include art and music and sculpture and architecture and philosophy as well—is so platitudinous as to have the force of novelty and so conservative as to demand some radical rethinking of what we are doing in general education. That thesis is the daring statement: the past is not the present. On the contrary, the past is significantly different from the present—that is why we study it, that is why it can be useful to us, and that is why it has meaning and imaginative charm. General education is impoverished when we neglect this central truth in an anxiety to prepare everybody for today's world—I apologize for the phrase, which is, however, now virtually technical—and general education can be enriched in proportion as this truth is understood. Tersely put, I remark that difference enriches; likeness palls. Perhaps I am saying no more than, as I have said, those who know no history are compelled to repeat it.

The centuries preceding this one did not consciously anticipate either the troubles or the triumphs of 1965. They were not at work shaping the administration of Lyndon B. Johnson. Alcibiades was not a premature McGeorge Bundy, nor Cicero an earlier version of Senator Dirksen. The present is, indeed, the child of the past, but as the current complaint is that parents do not understand their children, the argument is equally valid that children do not understand their parents. Preparation of life—that ancient slogan of the schools—is not especially helped by the assumption that the past is only a distorted mirror-image of the present, unless we are prepared to believe, as I am not, that the lesson of history is that history has no lesson.

I suppose that theories of history fall into three vast categories. First, in the Ancient East, inasmuch as time and matter are fundamental illusions, history, or what seem to be events, is so illusory as to be meaningless. A like doctrine is taught in the Book of Ecclesiastes in the Old Testament. Second, from the time of the Greeks to the time of Darwin, there have been historiographers, ecclesiastics, and metaphysicians who held that history is something over which man, the puppet of the goddess Fortuna, has virtually no control. This doctrine might turn out to be a cyclical version of history, as among the Greeks; or it might turn out in a crude sense to be a providential version of general decay or general damnation, as it was among the Romans of the Empire and the Christians of the Middle Ages; or it might be an optimistic version of history, as it frequently was among European deists who held that day by day in every way everything was getting better and better. From the time of Darwin to our own, a third theory tends to prevail; the doctrine that history runs in a sort of evolutionary spiral over which man, by virtue of his superior nature and nurture, has at least partial control. This doctrine, which finds some support in modern researches into genetics, tends to a cautious optimism and is the doctrine explicitly or implicitly taught in the schools, particularly in courses in world history, general history, or, sometimes, social studies.

What, now, are the uses of the past? I begin by noting that there is too much of it and that history perpetually grows as today becomes yesterday, and archaeologists extend yesterday indefinitely backward. In spite of this handicap, we try to teach the whole of history to adolescents, even though departments of history in our universities are satisfied if a promising doctoral candidate masters some minuter area in the vast empire of time. Obviously the idea that world history is possible in a single package is not new; Orosius, a Christian bishop of the fifth century, wrote a world history quite as sweeping as the high-school texts in that subject now in use. It is also true that reformers like Volney in the eighteenth century and H. G. Wells in the twentieth have written world histories, each in a single volume, the first devoted to the proposition that nations rise and fall and the second to the proposition that nations on the rise must be especially cautious lest they fall. It has remained for our time, however, to assume that adolescents can be exposed to so large a fraction of the intricate history of man as to make them love Latin America and support the United Nations.

I have not, of course, read all the textbooks in world history or general history now in use in the schools, but I have looked into enough of them to learn that they are not written for historians and are, in a sense, not written by historians. They are usually cobbled together by three inharmonious forces: textbook salesmen who in their quarterly meetings try to determine what will sell, school administrators who tend to the point of view that the teacher should imitate the radius vector of the planets and sweep over equal areas in equal time, and teachers of history, commonly two or three in number, who put the book together less for the sake of Clio than for the sake of cash. After a brief picnic with the biologists and with Cro-Magnon man and a stop-over among the Swiss lake dwellers, these texts begin civilization with the Nile Valley and the Fertile Crescent, transfer it to Greece, bow in the direction of Jerusalem, move on to Rome, travel northwest to France and Britain, and come to a full stop in the United States. This is done to check and cure a parochial point of view. The difficulty is, however, that it does not check it—it re-enforces parochialism. If you want to know why I say this, I ask you imaginatively to transfer this book to, say, Polynesia, whose explorers went out on voyages more daring than Columbus, before the time of Ferdinand and Isabella; or to any Buddhist country; or to a Mohammedan one. If these cultures seem remote, try it out in the school system of Israel. From the point of view of the Jews, the Nile Valley and the Fertile Crescent were enemy areas from which, in the providence of time, Jehovah let his people escape, the Greeks and the Romans were barbarous conquerors, and western Europe a prison-house centuries in the building and more or less cruelly administered from before the era of Justinian to past the age of Hitler.

Inasmuch as the education of high-school teachers of history, even if they have reached the master's degree, is bound to be less thorough than that of academic professors of the subject; and since in the universities professors of world history are extremely rare, one may legitimately inquire on what basis of historical interpretation and out of what fund of knowledge these world surveys are taught. There is no adequate fund of knowledge, and there is no basis of historical interpretation. These courses are fused with a division of high-school work vaguely called the social studies, and the teaching of world history often resolves itself into elementary problem-solving, the problems necessarily being problems like or relevant to those of today's world. A few samples will show what I mean. Although Mayan inscriptions still offer, I am informed, certain difficulties to linguists and archaeologists, the young son of a friend of mine recently discoursed eloquent music on the parallel between the numerical system of the Mayans and our own, reaching the not very surprising conclusion that both peoples had to learn to count. A young female relative of mine who knew nothing about either sailing or economic life talked before her peer group on the navigation of the Nile in ancient Egypt and its likeness to modern commerce. I believe it is not unusual to draw somewhat heavy-handed likenesses between democracy in ancient Athens and democracy in modern America, though, except that the word comes from the Greek, the only Greek democracy we ever attempted was that in antebellum South Carolina and its neighbors, the results of which were notably unfortunate. It is true that the idea of the Ku Klux Klan seems to owe something by way of Walter Scott and Goethe to the Vehmgericht of medieval Germany, but I find it difficult to see how any knowledge of the Ku Klux Klan, which must necessarily be vague, throws much light on medieval Germany, nor how any knowledge of the Vehmgericht, which must be even vaguer, throws any light on the operations of the Ku Klux Klan. Titles of papers or reports like "Benjamin Franklin: Entrepreneur or Humanist?" seem to me thoroughly misleading for three reasons. In the first place, in any modern sense of the terms Franklin felt no opposition between these values. In the second place, Franklin vigorously opposed the required learning of Latin and Greek in a century when a humanist was a man who was learned in Latin and Greek. And in the third place, the word "entrepreneur" did not come into the language until 1878, when it meant the director or manager of a public musical entertainment; it did not take on any economic overtones until 1885 when it came to mean an intermediary between

93

capital and labor; and at the present time, if the *Diction-ary of Social Sciences* is to be believed, there is no agree-ment as to what it means. I find it difficult to fit Poor Richard into any of these categories, though the peda-gogical intention is, of course, to be smartly up-to-date.

So far as it is an accurate exploration and objective restatement of what we can find out about a past that is perpetually falling into fragments, the aim of history is to be scientific; hence the epic dullness of certain great historical masterpieces like Stubb's *Constitutional History of England* and Henry Hallam's *Introduction to the Literature of Europe in the Fifteenth, Sixteenth, and Seventeenth Centuries.* But the great historians from Herodotus to Gibbon, from Voltaire to Henry Adams, from Macaulay to Samuel Eliot Morison have been liter-ary artists, concerned with narrative, with the drama of the past, with, as in the case of Carl Becker, the trenchant statement of a governing idea or set of ideas, or with a lively and vigorous, sometimes theatrical and often preju-diced, presentation of character, as in the instances of Froude's Mary of Scotland, Carlyle's Cromwell, and Sandburg's Abraham Lincoln. Being literary artists, they have not attempted a delineation of the universe. Even Gibbon, though his monumental work is in six vast vol-umes, confined himself to the decline and fall of a single empire; and Henry Adams was content to trace the for-tunes of the American Republic under the administra-tions of Jefferson and Madison.

I pause to quote from a very great and very prejudiced historian—perhaps his greatness arose in part from his prejudices—Lord Macaulay, who wrote in his essay on "History":

The perfect historian is he in whose work the charac-ter and spirit of an age is exhibited in miniature. He relates no fact, he attributes no expression to his characters, which is not authenticated by sufficient testimony. But by judicious selection, rejection, and arrangement, he gives to truth those attractions which have been usurped by fiction. In his narrative a due subordination is observed; some transactions are prominent, others retire. But the scale on which he represents them is increased or diminished, not according to the dignity of the persons concerned in them, but according to the degree in which they elucidate the condition of society and the nature of man. He shows us the court, the camp, and the senate. But he shows us also the nation.

Macaulay goes on to express his admiration of Walter Scott, to sketch a history of England on narrative and dramatic principles, and to conclude:

The instruction derived from history thus written would be of a vivid and practical character. It would be received by the imagination as well as by the reason. It would be not merely traced on the mind, but branded into it.

I confess that most textbooks in history received in the schools, at least so far as I have looked into them, are not vivid, are not narrative, are not dramatic, and brand nothing into the mind. Can it be that we are approaching the teaching of history wrong end to?

I fail to see the need of turning general education into a historical encyclopedia. I do not see that it is necessary to teach all of a subject to make a pedagogical point. These courses in world history or Western civilization or whatever other title they may have intend honorably. They seek, as I have remarked, to avoid parochialism by teaching universals. Surely, however, it is unnecessary to survey the development of all mankind to establish the truth that people were happy before the invention of television and troubled before the so-called "hell's angels" took off for summer resorts on their motorcycles. The drama of history does not lie in its endlessness, but in some compact story, some particular tragedy or triumph. It lies in contrast, not blur. Let us richly establish the truth that in some other place, and time, men, women, and children lived and died, sorrowed and enjoyed themselves, went on great adventures or invented great thoughts after fashions radically different from our own. To make this point shrewdly a single phase of history, if it be richly thought about, is infinitely better than all history thinly masking social problems.

For this purpose—that is, for the general purposes of education—any great age will do, provided that it differs dramatically from our own—the European Renaissance, the age of the Antonines, some great period in China, the Enlightenment, medieval times, Biblical archaeology, the spacious days of great Elizabeth. One does not have to survey the whole history of transportation to discover that the Romans half strangled their draft horses by putting ropes around their necks instead of attaching the weight to be pulled to traces hooked on to the bellyband that formed part of a harness fitted to the barrel of the animal. To comprehend the significance of Byron's characterization of Rome as lone mother of dead empires does more for the reason and the imagination than most attempts to vivify the republic of Julius Caesar by pretending it is the republic of Ulysses Simpson Grant.

The humanities, I repeat, are not the fine arts in modern dress but that part of general education in which the past can be made to come alive and to make its commentary on the present. I urge that we follow Thoreau's doctrine: simplify, simplify. One good course in the Renaissance, enriched by good readings, slide lectures on art and architecture, the playing of records will make the point far better than the vague blur of a course in Western civilization or world history—that is, if the point to be made is the point that I understand we want to make: namely, that other men and women in other times lived human lives radically differing from the lives of men and women living now. I think a teacher with enthusiasm for Renaissance culture—or for any other great period of culture east or west, north or south—will do more to correct parochialism if he is given his head than a whole battery of instructors laboring feverishly at the history of the world or a vast shelf of great books. Of course, some great books have to be taught—Shakespeare is one of them—but that does not mean we have to teach all the great books all the time. Of course, the class that concentrates on the Renaissance will not know very much about Chinese culture; but as I incline to believe courses in world history leave but imperfect memories of Chinese culture on the mind, I would rather release passion, enthusiasm, and special knowledge. I do not think we can train teachers of all the great books and of world history. I can, however, conceive of teacher-training programs matched with proper temperaments and interests that will make some single portion of the past vivid and dramatic; and in so doing, call into critical question, even among the young, the preoccupation of the present with the values of industrialism, advertising, and imperial power.

97

PEOPLES, AND NATIONS,
AND TONGUES

I BEGIN by cheerfully acknowledging my professional incompetence to discuss anything technical connected with the teaching of foreign languages. I was brought up in the Middle West during an anti-foreign language period, involving the banishment of German from the schools on the ground that it was an enemy tongue and created hyphenated Americans; and, what is worse, brought up in what is now regarded as an eolithic methodology. We had no informants, structural linguists were not as yet invented, teachers recognized the parts of speech as formularies logically differentiated from each other, and the foreign language books I was set to master were commonly literary works of some significance in the literature of the country speaking the language to which my infant or adolescent years were exposed. When I entered the graduate school I was required to study Old

This address was delivered before the Foreign Language Association of Northern California, meeting at Covell College, University of the Pacific, Stockton, California, on May 1, 1965, and was printed in the *Northern California Foreign Language Newsletter,* May, 1965. The title was suggested by the Book of Revelations 7:9.

and Middle English, and I escaped from Gothic only by some feat of administrative legerdemain I never fully understood. In those days Grimm's law had the sanctity of the constitution and rhotacism was a powerful and mysterious force operating on words we knew not how, we knew not why. I learned German, French, and Italian in this rudimentary way, and my later experience with these and other languages has been wholly literary: that is, I have translated works out of some ancient and a few foreign languages as an exercise in belles-lettres.

But last year, from January to mid-June, I was Paley visiting professor of English at the Hebrew University in Jerusalem in Israel. Except for the English department and, curiously enough, the medical faculty, teaching at the university is carried on in Hebrew. The reason why the medical faculty offers instruction in English as well as Hebrew is that English is the only tongue common to the many students from foreign countries, particularly the emergent African states, studying there to be doctors or nurses. But even these students, when the time comes to walk the hospitals as internes or to take care of patients, must learn enough Hebrew to communicate with those they care for. Surrounded therefore by a Hebrew-speaking nation and carrying on my own instruction in what is for the Israeli a foreign language, I was deeply interested in the language problem in that small, intense, and interesting state. The problem divides into two unequal parts.

The first part concerns Hebrew. By law, custom, pride, and necessity all the inhabitants of Israel who are in any sense citizens of the state, except the Arab minority, must learn to speak, read, and write Hebrew—not any kind of Hebrew, not kitchen Hebrew, nor lingua franca Hebrew, nor, if I may coin the expression, pidgin Hebrew, but the official Hebrew established by the state as a sign of national identity. Since under the law of the return, Jews emigrating to Israel from any part of the world and from local cultures where only the rabbi and a few Talmudic scholars may have mastered classical Hebrew, instantly become citizens, the necessity of establishing a common language was painfully evident. Immigrants came into the state speaking Yiddish, or Arabic, or French, or German, or Coptic, or some one of the Slavic languages, or Rumanian, or even Hindi—a whole Babel of tongues. They had somehow to communicate with each other. Those who could not read and write had to be taught to read and write some common language, and Hebrew was chosen. Yiddish, a remarkable dialect with a rich literature, was ruled out because of the cultural division its use might perpetuate.

An ancient tradition made Hebrew, difficult though many persons find it to master, inevitably the language of the Jewish state. Even before the creation of that state modern Hebrew had been invented or devised by a few far-seeing scholars. But the Israeli are the people of the book, and Hebrew had therefore the sanctity of age, of religious tradition, of race, and, in its classical form, of literary dignity. Modern Hebrew is policed by an Israeli academy, and though no language, I suppose, ever wholly submits to academic control, the influence of the academy, of books, magazines, and newspapers—and the Israeli are great devourers of the printed word—and of the cultivated men in government, the courts, the embassies, and other influential places, including of course the rabbinate and the university people, has been relatively successful, I am told, in maintaining Hebrew at a high cultural level. Of course, the language of the street and the playground is not that of the elite, and of course the necessity of adapting an ancient language to a modern industrial nation has created some odd terms. For example, the rear wheels of an automobile are known as the "backax" and the front wheels therefore logically become the "front backax." But this is not characteristic of the whole language. In Israel Hebrew is a living tongue of astonishing vitality. Its journalism is racy and good. Its humor is said to be excellent. Modern Hebrew literature is vigorous, subtle, and varied. I am informed by American legal friends who know Hebrew that pleadings before the courts there are comparable in elegance to pleadings before any American court.

The Arab minority retains its right to use Arabic, and to speak Arabic in the Knesset, or parliament. This necessity aside, however, every person settling in the state as a citizen must, if he is to occupy a post in government, teaching, or any like enterprise, learn Hebrew within a year of his coming, and for this purpose special schools are established, many of them day-long schools, so that the learner is saturated in Hebrew until it becomes second nature with him. And of course it is virtually impossible to carry on any profession or business without a mastery of the national speech.

The astonishing success of the Israeli in transforming an ancient tongue into a warm, pliant, vigorous modern language is a remarkable phenomenon. The success is explicable by two or three reasons. In the first place the identification of Hebrew with Israeli nationalism was inevitable in a state beset by a ring of hostile powers. It is simply impossible, for example, in modern warfare where instant decisions must be made, for the high command of the armed forces to have to translate these decisions into half a dozen languages without loss of precious time. A polyglot parliament would not do. The legal situation in Israel is extremely complex, for the courts have to deal with Turkish law, British mandate law, Arabic law, rabbinical law, Mosaic law, the statutes passed by the Knesset, and precedents from the common law of Great Britain and the United States, and to complicate this problem still further by polyglot pleadings would have been nonsense. Even if, to the outsider, the long-run practicality of reviving a difficult dead language spoken by no other nation in the world might be questioned, the outsider would be stumped to substitute anything else. It was Hebrew or nothing, and the attempt has been successful.

But the uniqueness of modern Hebrew, a language not spoken by other nations, has thrown upon the Israeli the necessity of learning a second tongue if they are to communicate with the rest of the world; and for this purpose English has become the commonest, though not the sole, secondary language in the state. But how shall this foreign language be taught? This is the second problem. Shall it be taught so that the Israeli students can read Shakespeare and Milton and Emerson and Whitman or shall it be taught on a practical basis of ordinary business communication? Opinion is deeply divided. The cultivated minority believes that English is a language of culture; another fraction of the population, excited by popular books in English, by radio, by the comic strips, by the movies, and by popular British or American journalism, finds Milton and Shakespeare less interesting than Jack Benny or the Beatles, and so the issue is joined. The issue is further confused by the question whether the English taught shall be American English or British English, and in the schools and the universities you can find a teacher from Great Britain or one of the Commonwealth countries carrying on instruction in a British or Scottish accent and another, who has learned his English in the

States, carrying on his instruction in the accent of Philadelphia or Chicago. I shall come back to this general
question.

I have touched only in passing upon one of the most
powerful reasons for the success of teaching modern Hebrew in the state of Israel. This is religion. Religion has
its special and intimate relation with the life of the Jews
not merely as a spiritual solace but as a total explanation
of history. What Christians call the Old Testament and
what Jews call the Bible is a central document in this
linguistic renaissance. It is not merely the chief store-
house of classical Hebrew from which modern Hebrew
could be derived, it is also, like the epics of Homer, the
history of the creation and purpose of a race. The stories
of Abraham and Isaac, of Joseph and his brethren, of
David and Jonathan, and all the rest; the drama of Job,
the poetry of the Psalms, the insight of the prophets, and
the records of the kingdoms of Israel and Judah have a
special meaning in a state that is reviving ancient Israel.
These materials are taught Israeli children in the kinder-
garten, repeated in the grades, reappear, enriched, in the
secondary schools, and become subjects and guides of
research for the faculty of Jewish studies in the university
and for archaeologists who not only find that archaeology corroborates the Bible but that the Bible is an authen-
tic guide to archaeology. For most of us, history begins
with the Egyptians, passes over to the Fertile Crescent,
moves on into Judaea, Greece, and Rome, and reaches its
climax in the United States. In the Israeli schools history
begins with Abraham, Assyria and Babylon and Rome
are for the most part forces hostile to the Jews, and the
European world is not a climax but a prison more or less
cruelly administered, out of which this ancient people,
guided by destiny, has at length escaped.

We have no American parallel to this literary and linguistic situation. If we were all members of the Mormon Church, and if the stories of Columbus and Captain John Smith, the Pilgrims and the Puritans, the American Revolution and the American Civil War were found only or principally in one book, to be confirmed or modified by archaeological evidence, we might have a parallel, but this is not our American case. The American constitution requires the separation of church and state, whereas Israel has no written constitution and the state springs from the religion of the people. We are not the people of the book and we have been under no obligation to revive and modernize Anglo-Saxon as a national language in order to survive in a hostile universe. Yet I suggest that the linguistic and literary situation in Israel offers certain useful suggestions about the teaching of language and literature in the United States.

If we are not the people of the book in the sense that the Israeli are, there was a time when both the British and the Americans regarded themselves as the Chosen People in succession to ancient Israel. It would be wrong to say that the very formation and enrichment of our language resulted from an increasing acquaintance with the Scriptures, but it is a commonplace of both literary and linguistic history that no other single element has had a more lasting effect upon that development. From King Alfred to T. S. Eliot, from Governor Bradford's *History of Plymouth Plantation* to the novels of William Faulkner, knowledge of the English Bible in some of its various translations, whether fragmentary or complete, has been central to the English vocabulary and to the cadence, precision, and color of English style. The great styles in English, like those of Wycliffe and Shakespeare and Milton, Donne and Dryden and Swift, and so on down through Dickens to Oscar Wilde and Thomas

Hardy have had their intimate relationship with the English Bible. Among the Americans Franklin, Emerson, Whitman, Melville, and Lincoln are similar instances. As with the Israeli, so, until recently, with the English-speaking world, whether as revelation in the case of Bunyan or as poetry in the case of Matthew Arnold, the Bible has been a dynamic center not merely of wisdom and episode, divinity and allegory, but also of style. Our ears were once attuned to it, the ears of our finest writers have been attuned to it, and until the present age of secularism, it has been one of the chief agents in maintaining both among the cultural elite and among the common people a standard of or feeling for style.

I do not for a moment suppose that in the United States in 1965 the Bible can be restored to the place it has in Israel or to the place it has had for writers as various as Shakespeare, Swinburne, Cotton Mather, and Abraham Lincoln. When it becomes necessary, as it is now necessary, to explain by footnote reference in college texts that titles like *The House of Mirth, The Wings of the Dove,* and *Absalom, Absalom* originate in an obscure translation of a book known as the King James Bible, no amount of preaching or teaching can restore this document to its original centrality. Students consult the Bible nowadays in the same way they consult a gazetteer or a dictionary—they "look things up in it," and that is that. Nor do I imply that by teaching the Bible we would now necessarily improve either the Americans' command of language as speech or their capacity to write it clearly and well. I am saying only that the Bible as a source of power over language in our culture has waned for so long a time as nowadays to be negligible, and as it has not waned in Israel, where it remains the wellspring of the national tongue.

Well, if we do not have the Bible, what do we have?

We have the great secular classics, English and American, many of which show a relation to the Bible, and these we teach with a pertinacity that increases as a function of our attempt to keep the reading habit a vital part of culture. By reading habit in this context I do not mean mere literacy, but rather the easy companionship with books that is the aim of humane education. We teach with pertinacity. We are so far successful that the English wing of the Modern Language Association is the largest portion of that considerable body and the National Council of Teachers of English numbers something like sixty thousand members. We are immensely concerned with methods of instruction, with methods of interpretation. But we teach, if you will forgive me, without much historical sense.

Every age re-makes the past in its own image to some degree, but we do not so much remake the past as ignore its pastness as something merely precedent to, and different from, the present time. We interpret the secular classics less and less as masterpieces reporting on human life in ways far more varied than we can achieve, and more and more as premature contemporary documents confirming us in our predilection for misery. We interpret many of these documents as social alienation, as frustration, as primitive expressions of Freudian or Jungian psychology, as prophetic expressions of our thirst for *Angst*. Does this seem an excessive statement? We have had Hamlet turned into a classic case of the Oedipus complex, *Huckleberry Finn* into a puberty rite, "The Rime of the Ancient Mariner" into a totem and tabu problem, and the humor of Dickens into a veiled confession of sexual guilt.

To accomplish this we have had to read our own meanings into literary works that perhaps did not have

106

these meanings; that is, we have had to blur our sense of style, or, if you prefer, our sense *for* style—that is, we have had to avoid discriminating among the great styles of literary periods. But when you thus weaken the sense of style, you also weaken a sense for language. Style is the morality of art. As T. S. Eliot once said, the spirit killeth, the letter maketh alive. The Bible having vanished as a central and ennobling power in style, the secular classics as we now teach them do not replace it as a wellspring of a sense for speech.

Our teaching of literature has many virtues. Its range and variety are great. Its passion for psychological interpretation may, indeed, yield deeper and more subtle meanings than our predecessors got from the same literary masterpieces. Possibly we have a juster sense of the primacy of deep emotional drives in the making of literature than did the generation of Matthew Arnold. It is also true that in their prime the New Critics seemed to regard the problem of style as one of the primary problems of criticism. I suggest, however, that, by and by, picking apart a poem word by word and phrase by phrase, however valuable as exegesis, became an atomistic exercise rather than a comprehensive one; and what has happened since the earlier vogue of the New Criticism is that this atomism has been redirected to techniques of psychology masquerading as communication, rather than to style as a formal quality and main element in great periods of culture. We seek the hidden meaning of metaphor, we turn plot into myth, we seek the expression of the unconscious in what seems to have been consciously planned. Whatever value lies in this approach, it does not concentrate on style; or rather, since I am not making a plea for formalist criticism *per se,* it does not leave the student with any persuasive sense that the way a thing is consciously said is quite as governing a consideration as the way the thing said unconsciously reveals something not rationally expressed. Even if we do not go in for this kind of psychologizing, but concentrate on treating everything from the sounds that dolphins make to the sounds that Shakespeare makes as communication skills, we mechanize language, we do not work towards understanding its subtlety, its fullness, its grandeur, its variety. "Language," wrote Horace Mann in his *Second Annual Report* as Secretary of the Massachusetts Board of Education—"Language is not merely a necessary instrument of civilization, past or prospective, but it is an indispensable condition of our existence as rational beings. We are accustomed to speak with admiration of those assemblages of things we call the necessaries, the comforts, the blessings of life, without thinking that language is a pre-necessary to them all. It requires two things, entirely distinct in themselves, to confer the highest attribute of human greatness;—in the first place, a creative mind, revolving, searching, reforming, perfecting within its own silent recesses; and then such power over the energy and copiousness of language, as can bring into light whatever was prepared in darkness and can transfer it to the present or the absent, to contemporaries or posterity."

Well, what have we done with the energy and copiousness of the English language? Mann goes on to quote Pericles on the need for an orator's forming a competent and copious style. Oratory was once a major linguistic art. The orator has disappeared as a distinct type of literary artist with the passing of the nineteenth century and the coming of radio, though we have occasional imitation oratory in the United States Senate. Instruction in public speech, however, is now directed against eloquence, against rhetoric, against style, the theory being that the best way to make a public speech is to pretend that you are not speaking in public. The painful quality of most American public addresses, their inadequacy both as exposition and as style, whether in politics or at a meeting of the Modern Language Association, would seem to be a direct result of this attitude.

The huckster voices on radio and television, vulgar and raw, or insipid and saccharine, are a second manifestation of the decay of style. Moreover, to say that you object to this sort of thing, or that it could be made better marks you as un-American. I note with delight, therefore, certain honorable exceptions to the general debasement of radio English, notably the language of news commentators like Edward Murrow and Louis Lyons. Theirs is an English efficient, molded, and frequently beautiful; but their achievement, alas, illustrates in a curious, upside-down sort of way the truth in Goethe's famous dictum: In der Beschränkung zeigt sich erst der Meister. The increasingly narrow band of time allotted to serious commentators amid the welter of advertising has forced clarity and economy upon them. But in a culture in which most public statements are ghost-written, most public statements are gray. Since Lincoln we have had nineteen presidents in the White House. To read their presidential messages and papers is, with rare exceptions, an appalling task.

Finally, it is to be noted that our reviewers of books, plays, music, and the dance are themselves usually without a style of their own or a sensitivity to style in others. If this judgment also seems severe, I ask you only to compare the reviews printed in any of our weekly magazines or in the Sunday papers with the theater criticism of William Hazlitt, the music criticism of George Bernard Shaw, or the weekly essays of Sainte-Beuve. A like lack of concern for style will, I fear, eventually be charged against many of our novelists. Hemingway aside, how many of them have achieved, or care about achieving, style in the sense that Jane Austen or Stevenson or Henry James or Thackeray labored at the stylistic problem? How many of their readers care? At a recent writers' conference one prominent fictionist, answering the question: "Why do you write?" answered with passion: "I write to find out who I am." This sounds like a crushing retort until you think your way through the real question: What *is* a work of literary art? Our novelists often write well, sometimes superbly, but they seem unable to sustain themselves for a length of time on a given artistic level. Their great and splendid passages are followed by imitation passages, so that in a book like *Look Homeward, Angel* or *The Naked and the Dead* you find magnificent episodes and credible characters, but the book itself too frequently substitutes garishness for gold. *The Sound and the Fury* is one of the stylistic triumphs of the age, but Faulkner, with no apparent sense of difference, was also capable of the muddy prose of *Pylon* and the false Gothicism of *Sanctuary*. There is an opening sentence of his in a shorter tale that wanders over a page and a half, jarring the ear and confusing the mind because it has neither syntax, cadence, nor necessity.

Well, retired professors always lament the decay of the world, and it is now time to ask what has all this about the state of Israel, what has all this about the decay of a sense of style, to do with teaching foreign languages in the United States? I reply that it has an immense importance in this context. As we continue to lower our feeling for style in this country—and the controversy over the latest edition of Webster's International Dictionary shows that the issue is not closed—we necessarily cheapen the feeling for language, we necessarily turn away from the doctrine that language is a noble instrument that can be used for noble purposes, to the acceptance of language as communication skills taught in language laboratories as ends in themselves. Language is an instrument of communication—true; machines in the laboratories help us to master the rudiments of a foreign language—true, but the point of including the modern foreign languages under the National Defense Education Act was, I suggest, neither an absorption with technological tricks for teaching it more effectively, though this is in itself excellent, nor the assumption that the kind of language taught need not rise above contemporary colloquialism. I do not know how it is with others, but when I speak to the waiter in French, he frequently answers me in English. So far as communication is concerned, we get along just as well as if we were both fluent in Japanese.

There is here, it seems to me, a confusion of means with ends, of performance with context. Probably the plausible and practical motive that brought the teaching of foreign languages under the National Defense Education Act was a memory of our unhappy experience in World War II when, in spite of the attempts of the American Council of Learned Societies to prepare materials and teachers in many languages, particularly the Oriental ones, we entered the war linguistically naked, and had to set up cram schools in all sorts of tongues to prepare officers and enlisted men to cope with everything from Arabic to Tagalog. I have no defense for our linguistic poverty, no desire to repeat the experience, and every sympathy with all our modern devices for improving the teaching and the learning of foreign tongues. But I submit that this is not the whole purpose of the act, and that a mere colloquial command of this or that foreign tongue is an insufficient defense of American culture. I am the more persuaded of my conviction when I reflect that in addition to language laboratories and summer institutes for teachers, we also set up and continue to support area studies in great foreign cultures; we continue to believe that a junior year abroad in France or Germany, Austria or Italy is an excellent thing; and we try through the United States Information Service Libraries scattered over the world, to persuade foreigners that American culture is more than jazz, tough detective stories, racial intolerance, and disguised imperialism.

I grant that many students in required courses in foreign languages will develop no literary sense, will not pass beyond a rudimentary vocabulary, and, what is even more depressing, will probably never have an emergent occasion to employ or improve what foreign language they may have been exposed to. I applaud the steps that are taken to enable us better to cope with a pedagogical problem totally different in kind from that in Israel or Switzerland or Denmark.

But the good is the enemy of the best, and I think it makes a great deal of difference whether we think of the problem of foreign languages and literatures in the context of communication skills or in the context of comparative cultures. I suggest that the relatively mechanical approach latent in the National Defense Education Act and, as some scholars think, in the Foreign Language Program administered by the Modern Language Association is neither the purpose of the one nor the aim of the other. I noted with interest in Israel that where the teaching of English was confined to colloquialism it was relatively unsuccessful, but where the sights were raised to include literature, mastery increased. There is, I grant you, some social difference in Israel as elsewhere between the families of children who never got beyond a primitive vocabulary in English and the families of those who feel that English is an important gateway to the culture of the Western world, but this argument is as broad as it is long; are we therefore to confine our foreign language work in the United States mainly to those who, unshaped by our own literary culture, are to remain impervious to any form of culture either domestic or foreign? Will the purposes of national defense be truly served by this argument?

We have been teaching Spanish in this country for a good many decades. Portuguese is still a relatively neglected tongue. We have also made repeated efforts, from the days of John Quincy Adams to the days of John Fitzgerald Kennedy, to persuade the countries south of the Rio Grande that we are not enemies but friends, even though we conquered and keep half of Mexico and insist that leadership in this hemisphere is our sole responsibility. I think there are more and richer courses in Latin-American history now than there were in Woodrow Wilson's time, when we had our latest quarrel with Mexico and the ABC powers tried to intervene. Certainly there are more such courses than in John Quincy Adams' era, for in that period there were none. But if anything is evident in American defense policy so far as the Latin-American countries are concerned, it is a lack of harmony, a lack of success in this leadership. It works sporadically if it works at all. And when as an amateur I ask myself why the Latin-American countries do not find us *simpáticos,* the answer seems to me evident; we approach them along lines that seem to us simple and natural—the economic motive, the technological motive, the defense-of-democracy motive—but we do not approach them along the line to which they would more warmly respond, and that is the line of respect for an older culture and an acquaintance with its legal system, its philosophy, its literature, its special racial situations, its religion, and its interpretation of words like democracy, personalism, humanity, and liberty. There is, indeed, a fashion among us not merely of denigrating the Spanish language, but of denigrating as well the literature written in the Spanish language in the countries south of us, classic books in those republics but unfamiliar to North Americans. As for the most enormous nation of them all, the vast republic of the United States of Brazil, Alfred A. Knopf is, so far as I have observed, virtually the only American publisher to believe that Brazilian scholarship is worth the attention of North American readers. But how can we announce, as we quaintly say, that destiny has burdened us with the leadership of democracy in the New World, not to speak of the world at large, without making some effort to find out something about the value systems of the countries we blandly announce we are going to lead and to protect?

I shall confine myself to the single case of the Latin-American world, though I confess that our knowledge of the Canadian culture to the north of us is scarcely richer, simpler though that problem in some respects may be. What is more important than my rightness or wrongness in these instances, though I think they are glaring instances, of complacency, is, I insist, the context of any approach to the problem of teaching the modern languages and literatures, including literature and language in English. The circumstances that made viable the revival of Hebrew in the state of Israel are special circumstances, and do not apply to our situation except perhaps indirectly with one exception, but the exception is important—it is the relatively high level on which the Israeli propose to maintain their national speech, their linguistic style. They insist there is a style in Hebrew, and they make valiant efforts to maintain it. May we not profitably recur to our own earlier notion that speech habits, oral and written, are not indifferent matters but connote a basic problem of style, not something merely to be labelled communication skills? Sixty years ago Henry James published his important essay *The Question of Our Speech,* a pronouncement which, I am sure, the professional linguist looks upon as the utterance of an amateur. From the point of view of linguistic science, yes; from the point of view of civilization, no.

If you find Henry James, Hebrew, and the Israeli problem about the teaching of English as a foreign language irrelevant or amateurish, let me waive all these considerations and return to the central thesis of my argument; namely, that language is not merely a necessary instrument of civilization, past or prospective, it is also one of the highest attributes of human greatness. The teacher of language must forever remember that he is working with one of the two or three principal instruments of culture, mathematics being another such; and if he has his moments of weariness or discouragement, which in the American situation must often come, let him reflect that, precisely as the first steps in addition or subtraction lead eventually to the vast structure of modern science, so the beginnings of instruction in any language, our own or another, are an initiation into all historical, literary, and philosophical culture, present or past. Let us not confuse the trees with the forest, the means with the aims, the method with the goal. We are humanists first and last, linguists only instrumentally, using books and machines but as a property or force towards civilization. Even in the best-equipped language laboratory we must remember with Wordsworth that poetry is still the breath and finer spirit of all knowledge, still the impassioned expression which is in the countenance of all science. Words, said another one of the romantics, are fossil poetry. I suggest that foreign words are also potential diplomacy, potential culture, and potential peace.

CAMPUS: ECHO OR CRITICISM?

A EUROPEAN university, at least on the continent, does not have a campus in the American sense. The University of Munich occupies some buildings on either side of the Leopoldstrasse, a great, broad thoroughfare built, one imagines, for military purposes. The structures on this splendid avenue are, except for the church towers, of uniform height and very harmonious as architecture. Indeed, if one did not know where to look for the university, one would have had trouble in locating it, so much do its buildings resemble the apartment buildings and other structures near them.

Until recently the University of Munich took no re-

I taught in the Amerikainstitut of the University of Munich shortly after the end of World War II; and, called upon to address the Conference of the National Association of Student Personnel Administrators while my Munich experience was still fresh in my mind, I cast myself in the role of a Man from Mars in order to compare and contrast the European and the American university. The part of my address here published appeared in the *Harvard Alumni Bulletin* for November 4, 1955. Some of the things I saw in 1955 have obviously a relation to campus disturbances in the 1960's. Copyright © 1965 by the Harvard Alumni Bulletin, Inc.

sponsibility for the life of its students, and even today it takes very little. That is to say, it has no dormitories, it has no fraternities, it has no student union, it has no cafeteria, lunch room, dining hall, or other place in which the university serves meals, it has no gymnasium and of course no stadium, it has no campus activities in the American sense of the term. Because of the abnormal conditions in post-war Germany the university for a time served cheap food to some of its students, and made a few inadequate gestures toward finding quarters in which these students could live. I am ignorant whether this innovation has been continued. Generally speaking, however, though there are student clubs and societies, all that we call college life and extracurricular activities, and the like, are not found at the continental university. Being a student at such a university can be pretty grim business. If, for example, a student falls ill, it is up to him, or his landlady, or his fellow-students to see that he gets taken care of. He has to forage for himself to find cheap restaurants and that second necessity of German life, cheap beer.

His morals, his finances, his study habits, his psychology are his own responsibility. He pays a fee for any courses he wishes to attend. The names of the courses are entered in a little book he carries with him, but whether he attends the course or not is entirely his affair. There are no course examinations in our terms; and no grades on course work, no warning notices, no dean's list, no election to Phi Beta Kappa or Sigma Chi. The assumption of both students and faculty, and of the government which supports the university and never interferes with its intellectual life, is that an academic education is an intellectual responsibility for adult persons. The emphasis is upon learning, not upon teaching; and the theory is that if anybody who has made sacrifices to go to the university or for whom sacrifices have been made, is childish enough not to take advantage of his opportunity, the responsibility for being a fool is his and not the institution's.

When the student decides he is ready to do so; when, in other words, he feels he has attended a sufficient number of lectures and been a member of a sufficient number of seminars, he may apply to the faculty under which he has enrolled—the philosophical faculty, for example, which corresponds in a rough way to our college of arts and sciences. He will show a faculty representative his little book, he will show a number of flimsy pieces of paper called *Seminarscheinen*—and it is his responsibility to keep them, not the registrar's responsibility—and the faculty, or a committee of it, will, if he has a case, examine him to see what he knows. If he satisfies them, well and good. If he fails, there are no make-up examinations, no excuses, no dean, counsellor, psychiatrist, personnel administrator, Y.M.C.A. secretary, or religious adviser to whom he can go. All he can do is to try again some other time.

Student life can be grim, as I say. One student of mine at Munich had only one shirt to his name; he slept, free of charge, in a coal bunker because he could not afford a bed; and he was trying to get along on one meal a day. Another man, attempting in our terms to work his way through college, had a night job and yet attended lectures in the daytime, so that he always fell asleep. I do not, however, wish to paint too dark a picture. Many students were in more comfortable circumstances, though nobody had very much money. The European university calendar leaves lengthy intervals between semesters, so that many students are able to earn money between terms and so stay in the university. But the competition is terrific because in Germany a university education is necessary for any white-collar job of standing, and everybody dreams of a white-collar job.

In the matter of recreation, everybody in Europe, I sometimes think, has a bicycle, and a few have motorcycles. It is customary for students by ones and twos and threes, by groups, by clubs, by whole companies, to cycle out of town into some one of the groves or parks nearby, where there is perhaps an inexpensive outdoor beer-garden and, unwatched by the dean of men or the dean of women, enjoy themselves. Others take walking trips. Some of the motorcycles are equipped with side-cars, but, side-cars or not, if the student can save up enough money for gasoline, which is expensive, he and his best girl may go bouncing off through the beautiful Bavarian countryside for an occasional holiday spin. There is no parking problem on the university campus, for nobody has an automobile, and all our elaborate regulations about student cars, student parking, and student parties are unknown.

I have no special brief for Germany and the Germans. So far as their present plight is concerned, they were justly punished, if you want punishment to take the form of destruction. I think there are a good many faults in the old German university system, which the conservative Bavarians have virtually restored, despite American pressure to alter it. But these are matters aside from my central point.

So far as the notion of a university is concerned, there is, I think, no great difference between the German universities and other continental universities from Bergen and Upsala in the north to Naples in the south. The teaching is frequently bad, the university is sometimes a façade from behind which the life has departed. But in Europe it is universally assumed that a university—and there are no colleges in our sense of the word—is a mature intellectual enterprise primarily concerned with preserving and extending knowledge and maintaining the great professional classes—scholars, scientists, lawyers, doctors, clergymen, and so on—without which no culture can survive. It has no traffic with ideas like the development of personality, or worthy social purposes, or learning by doing, or education for a changing world, or a variety of other slogans characteristic of American education. Cultures come and go, nations rise and fall, governments wax and wane—the university remains.

If we turn from life in a continental university to student life in America, we enter a totally different world, or so it seems to the Man from Mars. It is a world younger, more variegated, less geared to intellectual endeavor. It is an undergraduate world, whereas the European university world is a world for adults. Entrance into the American college, or so thinks the Man from Mars, despite all the fuss about grades and getting your lessons and the top percentile, and college boards and intelligence tests and personal interviews, is far, far easier than entrance into a German university, partly because there are no European high schools in our sense of high school; partly because the so-called *Abiturexamen*—that is, the series of examinations one takes at the end of one's life in the European Gymnasium to determine his fitness for further training—is one of the toughest examinations in the world; partly because, by law in many of our states, any graduate of an American high school has a right to enter the state university, whether he is qualified or not; partly because privately-supported colleges have to depend upon tuition fees if they are to have students, and upon students if they are to have tuition fees.

In the American academic world, despite a good deal of well-meant protestation to the contrary, the emphasis is on teaching, rather more than on either knowing or learning. No European university would dream of solemnly asking its students to rate professors as some American universities now do, in an effort to ascertain who is to be promoted and who is not. The Man from Mars can only marvel at the logic behind this concept of the intellect. A European faculty is a congregation of men who know—that is, of highly trained specialists. If you as a student wish to become an intellectual, it is up to you to become one, it is not the responsibility of the professor to be patient with your dullness or your mediocrity or your laziness, and thereby win votes. There, the student joins a community of scholars. He goes to learn. Learning is a lonely process, fundamentally asocial, despite all our easy talk about well-adjusted personalities.

The Man from Mars is therefore compelled to observe that American college life is distinguished from academic life on the continent by a special quality, and he ponders the attraction and weakness of this quality. I do not wish to paint too dramatic a contrast and I am aware that young people are young people the world over, even though the European student is commonly more mature than is the American student. European students are something more than grinds. Let us not forget that the greatest collections of student songs in the world are the German *Studentenlieder,* or that in foreign universities student political life sometimes boils up and boils over with a fury unknown on American campuses, so that from time to time a university has had to be closed by the government in power. But nevertheless, the emphasis in the one group is upon the intellectual life, and upon the life of social adjustment in the other group—that is, in the American colleges. The Man from Mars is naturally interested to analyze the significance of this fact.

The more he studies American undergraduate life, the more he finds a kind of national philosophy running through it. All these student activities, which engage the attention of your members—getting into the right fraternity, competing for a place on the college paper, editing the yearbook, participating in the glee club or the dramatic society, winning place on the varsity squad, campaigning for presidency of the student council, student dances, student love affairs, student dormitory life, student religious groups—what is all this but a copy in miniature of life outside the campus, its snobbery, its competition, its generalities, its notions of what the good life is, its democracy, its frivolity, its serious concerns, its kindliness? On the campus, religion makes no more noise, so to speak, than it makes in town, whereas athletics make a great deal of noise in both localities. Compare the attention given to sports in the morning newspaper and that in the alumni bulletin—the proportion is roughly about the same. Finding one's place in the college social world parallels finding one's place in the world outside. The Big Man on Campus has an odd resemblance to the business leader, banker, politician, or manufacturer in workaday life. Traditionally, the American campus is an echo, not a criticism, of American society.

I say "traditionally." Tradition in America is never very long. If you have read Henry Canby's *The Age of Confidence* or Van Wyck Brooks's *America's Coming-of-Age,* you have learned that in the nineties and later, campus life was about the only preparation the student could acquire for our competitive society.

The Man from Mars is not persuaded this is altogether

wrong. He is not persuaded that our college catalogues are mistaken in listing and describing the nature and activities of student clubs and associations before they get around to the dull business of listing courses and professors. Conceivably, he thinks, we have here a central idea in American education.

If so, it is something unique in the world. Its virtue is to permit the undergraduate to imitate and practise the kind of life American society has hitherto demanded of him—the world of middle-class values and accomplishments. On the campus by a process of trial and error he learns what he has to know to get on more effectively in the world outside, and in the shelter of the college his mistakes do not carry the penalties similar errors might exact elsewhere.

But if undergraduate life has its excellences, the Man from Mars notes that it suffers from an apparently ineradicable defect. It is merely imitative. It has no values of its own. Its imitativeness, its quality as play, become immediately evident, even to the adolescent, once the student leaves the undergraduate college to enter the medical school or the law school or the graduate school or any other professional institution. Though he may still tread the same ground as do his quondam companions, though he may enter the same classrooms and study under the same faculty, he has virtually disappeared from the life of the college. The challenge of professional training is, he finds, an adult challenge, and the mature student, though as a child he spake as a child, must now perforce put away childish things. Consider, as example, the life of the candidate for the bachelor of arts, and the life of the same student when, three months later, he becomes a candidate for a degree in law. Reality is now intellectual reality, not imitativeness, and the student discovers what the undergraduate world does not permit him to discover, that there are deeper satisfactions in life than being elected editor of the college paper. The American professional graduate schools have had to learn that the heart of training is the intellectual love of learning. Until that is discovered, nothing is discovered. Education is not the mere capacity to be taught, it is not running for campus offices or getting into the right clubs or basking in the factitious and fleeting glow of athletic fame. It is not dependence upon deans, councilors, psychologists, and tutors. It lies in the lonely capacity to learn. Looking over his shoulder, I can see that the Man from Mars concludes that the great problem before the country, educationally, is: How can we make the undergraduate colleges grow up? How can we gradually diminish this prolongation of adolescence?

Of course I do not know enough to answer my own question. The whole vast force of emotion among the alumni is against any such notion. The whole vast force of American tradition is opposed to it—consider how American fiction, how American movies, how American fashion magazines (like *Mademoiselle*), how American newspapers picture the American college. Consider the vast emotional patterns annually woven around American football, American basketball, and American track by writers for that most influential part of American journalism, the sports page. Consider the effects of our national sorority and fraternity systems, with their emphasis upon good fellowship, their vague Boy Scout appeal to middle-age alumni for funds. Consider the commercialization of textbooks, more and more determined not by the intellectual needs of the subject, but by the reports of traveling salesmen as to what the mass market will take, not what the class market needs. Consider also

—and forgive me for being rude—that a vast battery of deans and tutors, advisers and proctors, psychiatrists and personnel administrators, religious counselors, big brothers, big sisters, doctors, nurses, Y.M.C.A. secretaries, orientation weeks, vocational guidance weeks, employment offices—I mean no disrespect to any item on my list, any of which can justify itself, I am sure—consider that this vast battery, all directed towards the social adjustment of the student, inevitably moves away from intellectual originality toward accepting any present social norm as an inevitable norm.

Our system means that the normal student is the average student, that is, the student who continues to get his lessons, continues to celebrate the virtues of football victories, continues to exhibit that lingering adolescent love of anonymity called school spirit, continues to act as if his four years in college were a miraculous continuation of what he did from the ninth grade through the twelfth. Do I seem unkind? On behalf of my Martian friend I must again remind you that the moment our young friend steps into a professional school he drops all this as if it had never been. And I might also remind you that because of the commitment of the college to secondary and popular work rather than to primary and intellectual endeavor, the hardest task before any college president is to raise money for general college funds rather than for a dormitory, a football stadium, a student union, a college chapel, or a baseball cage, though the commitment of the college is not to the baseball cage, nor to social adaptability nor to marriage, nor even to the armed forces of the United States—the commitment of the college is, according to its catalogue and its faculty, to the intellectual love of truth.

I am permitted to quote from a letter by a keen-witted

graduate of an excellent woman's college in the East, the writer of which, since leaving college, has gone abroad. It was written in response to an appeal for funds from the college whose degree she holds. She tells the dean signing the letter:

"When I was a freshman you called me in and told me not to be so much of an individual. I was completely shocked by this, and still can't quite understand it. I would think that the whole point of going to college is to learn to be an individual, to learn to think clearly one's own thoughts, and to learn to compare and evaluate them with the ideas of others. Yet this is not what I learned at college . . . [instead] I learned to assimilate with the crowd, learned to work together with other girls on dorm functions, fashion shows, time-wasting social competitions, etc."

And a little later: "What is the end result of 'gracious living'? Should a person strive for it? I think [the college] should be ashamed of such a motto. . . . I sincerely hope that my own children will have a chance to get a real education, not just four years of let's-live-together, play-together-happily-to-our-own-advantage."

This is, if you like, one-sided, but I wonder whether it is any more one-sided than the dean's original letter, which appealed for support because the college was committed to gracious living?

In simpler times, the American college could afford to be one of the ways by which the confused and charming emotions of adolescence could be safely prolonged in America for some four delightful years. I suggest that it is now too late in the world's history for this dream of endless youth to continue. Doubtless no small part of your professional labors arises in fact from the truth that the undergraduate college of the twenties has already begun to change radically under the pressure of war and the draft. Doubtless also no small part of the need of psychiatrists in the college world arises from the increased tension between dreamy adolescence and the demand for more rapid maturation on the part of undergraduates. If this be so, I think the change, though painful, is healthy.

"Every day you lose will retard a day your entrance on that public stage whereon you may begin to be useful to yourself," said Jefferson, just as he said that "when your mind shall be improved with science," you can then "pursue the interests of your country." I think in a grim world the interests of our country require that the undergraduate colleges develop as soon as may be intellectual standards comparable in quality at least to those we accept without a murmur from professional schools; and though I may regret the gradual passing of the bright world of the college campus of the past, that world and the possibility of that world must inevitably give way under national demands for mature thought and a reasoned philosophy.

When as a nation we were a child, we could speak as a child and think as a child, but there comes a time—and the time is now—when we must begin to put away our pretty toys and insist that literature, art, science, and philosophy are not the mere subjects of lessons dutifully to be got, but weapons to master for survival in this great critical period of human history. We must put away childish things. We must, if we are to survive, go back to our European origins and realize that the world of scholarship is a world of men and women, not a world of boys and girls.

THE ONCE AND FUTURE
STUDENT

I N A very few moments they are going to confer degrees on you. At this late hour there is nothing you can do to stop it. You shall, in the language of the Apostle Paul, be changed as in the twinkling of an eye. Up to this fatal hour you have been students; you are about to be translated as by a magician's wand into alumni. Hitherto the university has been responsible for your welfare; in a few moments you will become responsible for the welfare of the university.

As students you have been living in a communal society run on the lines of Plato's republic. There have been guardians watching over you. You have been housed in approved structures, and you have been fed meals that, if they were sometimes more palatable than they were at other times, were always scientifically prepared in the matter of calories, proteins, and vitamins. If as students

This was the commencement address at the University of Utah in 1966. It was printed as a pamphlet for distribution among the graduates and other members of the university and later appeared in the November, 1966, number of *Alma Mater,* the official organ of the American Alumni Council.

you have conducted experiments in scientific laboratories, precautions have been taken against accident, the outcome of the experiment was often guaranteed beforehand, and the eye of Big Brother disguised as a laboratory assistant was always watching you. You have studied carefully chosen textbooks in the social sciences. The literary works you have been asked to read have been carefully chosen by professional experts in a good many languages; and the English prose you have been asked to write has been inspected by some watch-dog of our common tongue. If you have been exposed to such pedagogical gadgets as audio-visual aids and computerized solutions to human problems, this has come about only after painful searching of the heart by professionals. Your minds have been as carefully groomed as if you were younger companions of Socrates and your bodies as painstakingly improved, where possible, as if you were going to live in ancient Sparta.

As soon as you have received your diplomas this watchful care will cease and you will be on your own. But something else will happen. You will become of exceedingly great interest to the secretary of the alumni association. All universities have alumni associations run by trained and skillful directors, and I have no reason to suppose this university is without one. The first business of the alumni secretary is to get you to join up, and his second business is constantly to remind you that you owe something to this university. In my own institution the head of the alumni is, like Nimrod, a mighty hunter, but though he likes to bring down the biggest game he can find, he by no means despises the smaller fry.

Now it is a curious fact about American life that ever since Harvard College was founded in 1636, colleges and universities have been short of funds. It is the business of the alumni secretary to help find these funds, and some of the directors are very persistent at it. At my college, for example, the alumni association according to legend annually sent to a graduate whom I shall call John Smith an appeal for contributions. In the course of time John Smith grew exceedingly weary of the yearly letter, and he once wrote across the face of the envelope "Deceased" and returned it to the alumni office, thinking this would end the matter. Not at all. The appeal appeared next year, addressed this time to the estate of John Smith, deceased.

The relation of the alumnus to his alma mater is, then, likely in the first instance to be financial, even in the case of institutions supported by public taxation. But no alumni secretary worth his salt stops with that. If we are to believe Thomas Carlyle, a cash nexus between man and man is never an enduring human bond. The alumni association of this or any other institution is only the outward and visible form of an inward and spiritual grace. These associations, these secretaries, and the universities to which they are attached come more and more to realize that an annual philanthropic gift is a poor tie between an institution and its graduates. The institution is, after all, an intellectual institution, not a gymnasium. The university-alumni relation has therefore two components beyond the financial one. These are relations of emotion and relations of intelligence.

The emotional relation between the American alumnus and his alma mater takes on a unique and national flavor that puzzles Europeans. The European university graduate does not lack a continuing interest in higher education, but his emotional tie is more characteristically with a distinguished scholar or scientist under whom he has worked than it is with an institution. In the United

States things are otherwise. Special circumstances governed the development of higher education in this country. Our colleges and universities sometimes began as academies and sometimes began as colleges; the university elements were added later. As a consequence the American campus life is in normal times unique. Student expressions of attachment to American institutions take form as singing the Alma Mater, chanting the college yells, and adopting a color or colors that become in time the official insignia, ranging all the way from Harvard crimson, which first blossomed at a boat race, to the pink and green of the University of North Dakota. These expressions of what used to be called school spirit, which is somehow different from the spirit of a school, do not always disappear upon graduation. College alumni revert to their youth at two Dionysiac academic festivals—the homecoming game in the fall and the class reunion in the spring, when highly respectable businessmen have been known to put an antic disposition on and cut capers that occasionally embarrass the police.

But the deeper attachment of the alumni to a university goes beyond the desire to get rid of a losing football coach and have a radical professor fired. The maturing graduate eventually discovers that he has been nourishing secretly and against all consciousness a richer, stabler, and more rewarding emotional attachment to the university. Some alumni, of course, fall by the wayside—our educational seed occasionally drops on stony ground—but an increasing number of university graduates everywhere in the country come to see the importance of and to cherish a tradition and an ideal. Both the tradition and the ideal have special reference to a technological culture.

The tradition is that of the continuity of learning across time. As American society becomes increasingly complex, learning—that is, the ordering of knowledge—takes on increasing importance in relation to the city, the commonwealth, and the nation, to business and industry, to public health and public policy, to religion and education, and to much else beside. We have in fact become so used to the borrowing from universities of experts in science, economics, sociology, and so on by the national, state, or local government that we do not realize how appalling this sort of thing would have seemed to Andrew Jackson, who honestly believed that any male adult of the right political persuasion could fill any office from that of the president to that of the village postmaster. We no longer shudder at the thought of what used to be called a brain trust in Washington; all our presidents from Herbert Hoover to Lyndon Johnson have called in special advisers from the academic world. What is true of the federal government is true also of state governments and of city administrations.

Attachment to a university fuses therefore with the concept of public need and patriotic necessity. A phrase like "Princeton in the service of the nation" is true not only of Princeton but of almost every other institution as well. Looking through the annual catalogues of the University of Utah, I read whole pages describing the channels by which effective knowledge gained in the university is poured into municipal, state, federal, and even international areas. The good of the university becomes one with the good of the nation; and the responsible citizen learns by and by that need in one area requires loyalty in another.

The ideal is of course the belief of administration, faculty, alumni, and the student body—even the most dissident part of the student body, which is vociferous in expressing dissatisfaction with the university, in one sense verifies the university ideal—the ideal is, I say, the notion that with proper support and sympathy a university can be made as the years go by to approach more and more nearly to the condition of being that perfected house of intellect of which Jacques Barzun has written. Whenever this idea spreads widely among the alumni, the growth of the university is assured: witness the histories of Harvard and Yale, Cornell and Oberlin, the University of Virginia and the University of Michigan among others. At this, the final stage of development in the attachment of graduates to institutions the emotional tie and the intellectual tie become one thing. The legislature of this state proudly supports the University of Utah but, as is commonly true of maturing institutions, I note that only one-third of the annual cost is met by legislative appropriation and that another third comes from gifts, grants, and research support. This important third is evidence that in proportion as universities ripen, an understanding of their highest function permeates the alumni.

But as I remarked a moment ago a mere cash relation between institution and graduate is a frail tie. It can be broken at any moment by a disgruntled graduate or group of graduates who think that this or that faculty member is a dangerous fellow or this or that university policy is wrong-headed. Such dissidents hope by force of numbers, political pressure, and above all the withdrawal of money that they can compel the university to alter its policy or dismiss the offending professor. Not so many decades ago, to take an extreme case, the entire economics faculty of a state-supported institution in Kansas was dismissed because they approved the free coinage of silver.

Universities are not always right, nor are alumni always wrong. University faculties like other professional bodies—for example, the American Medical Association and the American Institute of Architects—number among their members representatives of the right, representatives of the middle, and representatives of the left. So far as the humanities go, I agree with Emerson that librarians are not necessarily wiser than other men. So far as the social scientists go, I should not like to live under a government administered only by the Brookings Institution. So far as the scientists go, I have observed among them no greater wisdom than I have seen in other professional groups. Protesting alumni often have a case. But the case must be a rational one, not one of propaganda or passion. The university is justified in retaining odd or radical persons on its staff for the simple statistical reason that the majority of the faculty will never be either oddballs or radicals. As in all other professions, so in the university world: scholarly discipline produces so wide a spread of caution and objectivity that I have heard one experienced president say he wished he could hire a specimen communist so that the university could find out what a communist is really like. I need scarcely point out that propaganda forms no part of higher education, or that the student works not under one professor only but under thirty or forty. You will not as alumni do the university any good by assuming that Professor A, whose view you do not like, is so powerful that his teaching wipes out all the influence of Professor B, C, D, and E.

The attachment of alumni to the university is not, then, directed to making the university conform to this or that political view, economic measure, or special philosophy. It is rather directed to the support of an institution essential to the well-being of the nation and of mankind. Being human organizations, universities make their mistakes; they sometimes hire the wrong people, they sometimes embark on wrong policies. We do not remedy these errors, however, by marching the army in as they have done in Argentina, or by allowing students to bar out the head of the institution as they have recently done at the University of Mexico, or by permitting the student body, or some fraction of it, to occupy and hold administrative buildings as has happened at Berkeley, Chicago, and City College, New York. These are passional, not intellectual. Alumni relations should never be like this.

No, in the house of intellect issues are, or should be, thoughtfully weighed, not emotionally prejudiced. Amidst the clash and clatter of propaganda in our age the university should remain aware of, but a little apart from, any burning and tumultuous issue. Its business is to be concerned with actuality amid tumult, but its concern should be a serene concern. Its instruction, even at the freshman level, is instruction, however imperfect, in serenity. What that instruction does is to reveal a world of intellectual order. In a secular sense the university idea is that set forth in Tennyson's *In Memoriam*:

> Our little systems have their day,
>   They have their day and cease to be;
>   They are but broken lights of Thee,
> And Thou, O Lord, art more than they.

The scientist, however hard-boiled he may seem to many, has a secret sentiment for order and constantly seeks it, whether he is dealing with quasars or microbiology. Economists and sociologists and political scientists, however engaged in particular problems, measure their researches and their teaching by hidden patterns of perfection. The historian perpetually hunts out some understandable mode of explaining behavior across the centuries. The humanist, if he be a philosopher, seeks a

136

governing principle, pattern, or organizing idea for experience, and if his concern be with one of the arts, measures literature or painting, sculpture or music by some formula of idealism even when he puts high value on the irrational and the absurd, and denies every tenet of Plato and John Ruskin.

In sum, the university is neither buildings, nor men, nor acreage, nor programs, nor money, nor administration. It is the local and specific embodiment of a universal dream that began before Egypt and will continue as long as the life of man. That dream is a dream of a world in order. Men have thought about order in a hundred different ways—the order of pure ideas with Plato, the mathematical order of Pascal, who said that God geometrizes, the theological order of St. Augustine, the evolutionary order of Lyell and Darwin and Spencer, even the universe as a dying order with Henry Adams and the universe as eternal recurrence as with Nietzsche and with certain living astronomers. The search is endless but the quest is not futile. You have, to take a homely illustration, but to compare plumbing in the United States with the total ignorance of sanitation in tenth-century Europe. We continually establish guard houses along an endless path. Though the university is not the sole agency to do so, it is still the principal agency by which we endlessly push back a little farther in each generation the frontiers of ignorance. As students in this university you have had some glimpse, however imperfect, into the ways by which knowledge is won and transmitted down the endless generations of man; and as alumni your primary allegiance must be to the concept of the university as man's perpetual bulwark against intellectual anarchy, the living institutional symbol of what William Faulkner meant when he said in his Nobel Prize address that in the long run man will prevail.

THE
HUMANITIES
AS
INTERPRETATION

THE BIBLE FROM A LITERARY
POINT OF VIEW

A̶fter Saul had been secretly anointed by Samuel, he started home and on his way met a company of prophets whom, to the astonishment of those who knew him, he instantly joined. The people said to one another: "Is Saul also among the prophets?" Considering my total lack of status in this company of biblical specialists, I have read with peculiar interest the tenth chapter of I Samuel, in which the incident is recorded.

My commission, as I understand it, is to avoid specialism and to discuss the Bible from the literary point of view—that is, as a book for readers. I will not say for ordinary readers, since the ordinary reader reads the Bible, or reads in it, not as literature but as revelation, a point of view that virtually negates the literary problem. I assume that those who requested these papers had in mind that minority of readers who care passionately

This paper is one of five essays read at the 1960 annual meeting of the American Council of Learned Societies and published by that body in 1960. The other four addresses were by biblical or archaeological specialists; hence the allusion in the opening paragraph of this essay.

about art, who are sensitive to its values, and who have in Dr. Johnson's sense a tincture of letters which leaves them unsatisfied with a jig and a tale of bawdry. (I do not refer to either *Lolita* or *Lady Chatterley's Lover*.) My mandate is to discuss the Bible as a work susceptible of literary evaluation, not as an infallible scripture, a quarry for proof texts, a source for creed, church, or political policy, or guide or occasion for linguistic scholarship and archaeology.

Even this is a large order, and the first necessity is to reduce the problem to size. I shall therefore confine my remarks to the Bible in English. Great and powerful as the influence of the Bible has been in the original tongues or in other languages—the Vulgate and Luther's Bible are instances—we cannot in this small scope discuss this protean, this universal life. Here the English Bible must suffice and, furthermore, a particular Bible, the so-called King James Bible of 1611, to which we are forever in debt, Protestant, Catholic, Jew, and agnostic alike. In our English-speaking world the King James Bible is the central version. All previous translations, including that of the incomparable Tyndale, flow into it, and all subsequent versions flow out of it, whether they are revisions, simplifications, modernizations, or competing translations such as the Jewish Old Testament of 1917 or the Catholic New Testament of 1941. Their editors or compilers wisely retain so much of the haunting felicity of the King James Bible as their commitments to simplicity or scholarship or creed allow. For example: in the King James text the second verse of Genesis reads:

> And the earth was without form and void; and darkness was upon the face of the deep. And the Spirit of God moved upon the face of the waters.

In Rabbi Leeser's version as revised by the committee of the Jewish Publication Society this reads:

> Now the earth was unformed and void, and darkness was upon the face of the deep; and the spirit of God hovered over the face of the waters.

This retains twenty-five of the twenty-nine words of the earlier translation. Again: a familiar and majestical verse in the Apocalypse (Revelations 20:13) reads in 1611:

> And the sea gave up the dead which were in it; and death and hell delivered up the dead, which were in them; and they were judged every man according to their works.

The Catholic New Testament of 1941 reads:

> And the sea gave up the dead which were in it, and death and hell gave up the dead that were in them; and they were judged each one, according to their works.

The differences are trivial, the likeness obvious, extending as it does to the retention of the grammatically interesting "their works" of the King James version where a precisian might insist that every man is to be judged according to his works and his works only. Casual reading in other later versions, including the Bible in basic English, will reveal that they keep as much as possible of the rhythm, vocabulary, and structure that gave us the "great organ-tones" of the Jacobean masterpiece. Why not? If the King James Bible be, as it has been called, the noblest monument of English prose, it is idle for revisers to pretend that they never heard of it. There is a holiness of beauty no less than a beauty of holiness, neither of which is a monopoly of the Anglican church.

But if we agree upon the centrality of the 1611 Bible, we are still embarrassed by the vagueness of the terminology we must use. It may seem surprising that I now insist that "Bible" is an ambiguous word. I do so not because it has been used ambiguously in these papers, but because in common thought, in common speech, in education, and in literary history it is thought about as a book, not as a collection of documents of varying merit. Thus the famous phrase about the Bible as the noblest monument of English prose refers to a single volume which, if it patently lacks the aesthetic unity of, say, *Madame Bovary* or *The Red Badge of Courage* or *Paradise Lost,* has or is assumed to have at least the unity of Whitman or of Shakespeare.

We know that the Bible does not have aesthetic unity, that it is a library, an anthology of varying, disparate, and often contradictory documents, some written in one language, some in another—documents, moreover, that more often than not lack structural unity in their own right. The parallel of Whitman, the parallel of Shakespeare simply will not do, it is not a governing parallel, since, whatever the confusion of elements in *Leaves of Grass* or Shakespeare's plays, we feel in these books everywhere the controlling influence of a single personality. But the Bible was produced by writers living in distant and scattered centuries and dispersed to various lands, writing mainly in Hebrew, sometimes in Greek, the Hebrew usually classical Hebrew, the Greek being sometimes not very good Greek. These writers, moreover, were prophets, lawyers, historians, tragic poets, apostles, compilers, mystics, bards of erotic love, fictionists, and even, in the case of Proverbs in the Old Testament and of Ecclesiasticus in the Apocrypha, forerunners of Benjamin Franklin. The last part of this collection is rejected by the

Jews, the middle part is rejected by most Protestants and some Catholics, and about the arrangement of books in the first part Jews and Christians do not agree.

We as scholars know these things with our heads, but we do not know them with our sensibilities, just as we do not really care that the witches scenes in *Macbeth* may not be by Shakespeare. *Macbeth,* we feel, is all of a piece, and the same thing, we deeply feel, is true of the Bible, with the important difference that we read *in* the Bible, not *through* it, and vaguely transfer the quality of some great passage like the thirteenth chapter of I Corinthians or the twelfth chapter of Ecclesiastes to the book as a whole. The great, the incomparable power of the Bible is the power of style, a power so great, if I may say so, as to conceal the lack of architectonics, veil the disharmonies evident in particular books, and divert from view the impossibility of taking seriously the allegorization of The Song of Songs or Judith into theology.

If the word "Bible" is thus ambiguous, the term "literature" is endlessly confusing. In the world of literature there is a perpetual war in our members. What is incomparable art to some of our rarefied literary quarterlies is pedantry to the common reader; what satisfies *The Saturday Review* rarely satisfies the New Critics. It would be jejune to labor the point. We talk about literary thought, by which I suppose we mean the expression of thought in literary form (except when we mean something else), but we do not know what we mean by this phrase, or by literary criticism, or literary interpretation, or a literary point of view. If it be true that literature is the best words in the best order, the telephone directory, clear, succinct, and incomparably organized, is a masterpiece of expository statement. If my example seems outrageous, consider that Anglo-Saxon riddles, rules for a nunnery, a rhymed geography of England, abecedarian verses, the Strassburg oaths, and treatises on cooking have at one time or another been classed as literature.

If it is difficult to define "literature" and "literary," we can at least, so far as our present task is concerned, make clear what a literary approach to the Bible is not. Here is a paragraph of prefatory matter from the British edition of a Gideon Bible that I read last summer in London:

> The Bible contains the mind of God, the state of man, the way of salvation, the doom of sinners, the happiness of believers. Its doctrines are holy, its precepts are binding, its histories are true, and its decisions immutable. Read it to be wise, believe it to be safe, practice it to be holy. It contains light to direct you, food to support you, and comfort to cheer you. It is the traveller's map, the pilgrim's staff, and the Christian's charter. Here Paradise is restored, Heaven opened, and the gates of hell disclosed.

I admire this forceful, if mannered, rhetoric, which takes us back to the prose of the School of Charlemagne and which succinctly says what the Bible means to the devout. But if all the doctrines of the Bible are holy, all its precepts binding, all its histories true, all its decisions immutable, all literary considerations are irrelevant, just as they are in the case of congressional legislation, which fulfills its obligations to literature if it says what it means and means what it says. From the point of view of the Gideon preface, Matthew Arnold went wildly astray when he found the key to the Old Testament in righteousness and the key to the New Testament in spiritual rebirth. From the point of view of the preface, literature has no task to perform, but only theology, whose duty it is to look up precedents and reconcile conflicting passages as lawyers prepare briefs for a court.

Among other difficulties concerning literary judgment is the traditional organization of the English Bible. Not only is the text mechanically divided into numbered paragraphs called verses, but "verses" in this context has nothing to do with prosody although the originals are sometimes poetry and sometimes prose. These verses, sometimes splitting in the middle of a sentence, are then arbitrarily assembled into chapters, but the chapters have virtually nothing to do with the organic structure of the book. Finally, the books of the Bible are themselves in a majority of cases arbitrary constructs also, great exceptions like Job being among the more powerful parts of the whole. In the Old Testament particularly, narrative and legislative materials split in two, duplicate and parallel each other, or postpone to a later book the conclusion of an earlier one. Thus if at the end of II Kings you wonder why it is important to know that Jehoiachin, the king of Judah, ate bread before Evil-Merodach, the king of Babylon, you must turn to the end of II Chronicles or the opening of Ezra to find out. Thus also the two parts of Samuel and the two parts of Kings, if scholarship is to be believed, originally formed a continuous narrative; yet chapters twenty-one through twenty-four of II Samuel are a tenuous appendix upon the narrative.

Modern versions seek to avoid these arbitrary difficulties, printing a continuous text and distinguishing prose from poetry, but they cannot banish the medieval formulae which reappear in the margin. Moreover, every Sunday the ancient pattern is revived in a Christian church when the preacher announces his text. We know how all this came about, but so deeply engrained is the general belief that these divisions are quintessentially biblical, it is difficult for even intelligent laymen to comprehend that the Bible is a huge and colorful mosaic, that its units are not verses, chapters, and books, but parables, narratives, essays, fables, orations, lyric poems, statutes, love stories, historical records, biographies, and the interminable exhortations, scoldings, promises, and pardons of a God who is sometimes a *deus absconditus* and sometimes a personage like the gods in Homer, who takes sides and interferes in the affairs of men.

This shocks the sensibilities of many. Perhaps we of the Western world cannot view this volume as literary. We offer courses in the Bible as literature, but they are misnamed. We can no more ignore the fact that in our civilization the Bible is composed of Sacred Writings than a Muslim can regard the Koran as just another book. Try to discuss the Old Testament in the same way one discusses the Old Norse sagas or try to deal with the family life of Jesus as one deals with the family life of the Karamazovs, and the impossibility is evident. Even if one rejects the whole Christian system as a form of myth, to Americans and to Europeans Christian mythology is a thing apart, it cannot be confounded with Greek myth or Germanic myth or the myths of the Algonquin Indians, just as the dimensions of a figure like Moses or Jesus forbid us to discuss him as one might discuss Arjuna or Beowulf or Hiawatha.

Nevertheless and obviously, the Bible is one of the great primary books in Western literature. The only other members of the class to which it belongs are Homer and the Greek tragic poets. I exclude Plato for the reason that the method of the Bible is not the method of Plato; I exclude the Norse sagas, the *Niebelungenlied* and the *Chanson de Roland* despite their heroic qualities because, while it would be wrong to say that ethical considerations are absent from these works, ethics in them is not touched with religion to the degree or in the manner of the Bible. The Koran and the other Sacred Books of the East need not here concern us; and other great wisdom books of the West like the *Meditations* of Marcus Aurelius, the *Imitation of Christ,* or the essays of Montaigne either derive from the Bible, touch human life more thinly, or are otherwise clearly inferior.

The chief components of a great work of literature would seem to be theme, outlook, persons, figure, and style. The uses to which these components are put and for which they combine we call narrative, drama, lyric, meditation, exposition, persuasion, denunciation, and humor. The Bible contains abundant examples of all these, but fewer of humor than of the other kinds. Yet humor is not lacking. Do you suppose, wrote Oliver Wendell Holmes the elder, that no smile appeared on the bearded lips of the apostles when Jesus said of Peter, "Upon this rock (*petram*) will I build my church?" Wit is also an attribute of Jesus, as when he stopped dispute with the epigram: "Render unto Caesar the things that are Caesar's and unto God the things that are God's" and with another epigram: "Let him who is without sin among you cast the first stone." Humor of character and situation is not lacking, as when, in the wilderness, remembering the cucumbers, melons, leeks, onions, and garlic of Egypt, the people complained that now they had nothing to eat but manna, Moses in disgust rebuked the Lord: "Wherefore hast thou afflicted thy servant? and wherefore have I not found favor in thy sight, that thou layest the burden of all this people upon me? . . . have I begotten them, that thou shouldst say unto me, Carry them in thy bosom, as a nursing father beareth the sucking child . . . ?" The Lord, abashed, brought quails by a wind from the sea and let them fall near the camps; then, while the flesh was yet between the teeth of the Hebrews, he smote that people with a very great plague.

The themes of the Bible are simple and primary. Life is reduced to a few basic activities—fighting, farming, a strong sexual urge, and intermittent worship. With these must be associated death, friendship, and politics, the last being commonly without morals. From the quantitative point of view, three central subjects emerge, are endlessly iterated, and amount sometimes to monotony and sometimes to sublimity. This threefold theme is the interest of God in man, the wrath of God, and the weakness or rather the wickedness of humanity. The instinct that leads fundamentalists to regard the Bible as an inerrable message from heaven is in a literary point of view so far justified that the nature of God is central to the collection. The development, attributes, desires, frustrations, and penitence of deity are everywhere foremost and overshadow the actions of men from the first chapter of Genesis to the final phrase in Revelations.

For centuries scholars and theologians have struggled to interpret and unify the personality of God as thus set forth. Only since the development of historical scholarship have they dared to speak of Yahweh, Elohim, the tribal deity of the Hebrews, the contributions of the Canaanites, the parallels from Babylonia, and the concept of God's development. Because of the basic position of the Bible in Jewish thought and Christian theology, it is impossible to discuss the character of God in the Bible from a literary point of view as one can discuss the God of *Paradise Lost.* If one assumes with systematic theology that all the words, motives, and actions attributed to deity in the thirty-nine books of the Old Testament, the twenty-seven of the New, and the fourteen of the Apoc-

rypha refer to the same Ineffable Being, God in the Bible
becomes so complex as to destroy my observation that the
themes of this volume are simple and primary. To the
theologian this complexity may be a proper conception of
deity. The literary historian, however, must note that the
Lord of the Pentateuch is cruel, arbitrary, repentant,
kind, powerful, and helpless in the space of a single book
and that it is impossible to reconcile a deity who cannot
keep order in even the small Hebrew nation with the
majestic God in Job, the sympathetic father of Psalms,
the loving God of the New Testament, and the transcendental showman of the Apocalypse. If, however, we
take the appearances of deity distributively, each as its
immediate value, by itself, and without reference to consistency or system, we remain within a universe of discourse wherein everything is grand, simple, and primary,
as I have said.

This elemental quality in the themes of the Bible is at
once ground and occasion of a life and outlook quite as
primary as and often more primitive than that in Homer
or the Greek tragic poets. We confront basic virtues and
primitive vices. Men are brave, potent, loyal, faithful,
devout; they are fearless or frightened; they are cunning,
sensual, idolatrous, cruel, hypocritical. Women group
themselves into elemental categories—harlots like Rahab,
heroines like Judith, housewives like Sarah, Ruth, Re-
becca, and Mary the mother of Jesus, whom we see only
in her maternal role. The world these persons inhabit is
stripped and elemental—sea, desert, the stars, the wind,
storm, sun, clouds and moon, seedtime and harvest, prosperity and adversity, famine and plenty. In the third
chapter of Ecclesiastes we learn that to every thing there
is a season and a time to every purpose. Then follow
twenty-eight such times in balanced pairs which reduce

human life to its elements; as, for example, a time to seek and a time to lose; a time to keep, and a time to cast away.

Occupation has this elementary quality also: Nimrod is a hunter, Jehu a charioteer, David a shepherd, and the twelve apostles are mostly fishermen who correspond in the New Testament to the antique pastoral simplicity of Abraham, Jacob, and Boaz in the Old. Warfare is frequent and savage. Resistance is the utmost, victory is commonly pitiless, the vanquished are massacred or enslaved, cities destroyed, treasures plundered. Bravery has epic simplicity as in Homer: one thinks of David and his sling. One remembers these warriors for simple things— Joshua rending his clothes for shame after the defeat at Ai, the cunning of Gideon, the gigantic strength of Samson. As in an Eastern fairy tale, vast armies overwhelm the tiny state, which is subdued not so much by superior force as because the Lord has mysteriously decided to punish his people again.

Wealth is visible, tangible, edible: Joseph gives Benjamin three hundred shekels of silver and five changes of raiment and sends his father twenty asses laden with the good things of Egypt, among which are corn, bread, and victual, proof alike of his domestic affections, his political success, and his notions of the good life. We read in I Kings that "Solomon's provisions for one day was thirty measures of fine flour, and threescore measures of meal; ten fat oxen, and twenty oxen out of the pastures, and a hundred sheep, besides harts, and gazelles, and roebucks, and fatted fowl." Why not? The earth is the Lord's and the fulness thereof, and in such a world eating, drinking, and the engendering of children are natural goods, as remote from the tortuous sexual psychology of Proust as they are from the subtleties of Keynesian economics.

Numbers are naïvely exaggerated—it is impossible, even in the light of modern archaeological research, for Palestine to have supported these hundreds of thousands, who are counted by rumor only. The biblical world is a world of myth, taboo, folklore, tradition, racial hatreds, natural wonder, elementary emotions and adoration, a world in which from time to time and eventually a few great souls—the authors of the Psalms, of parts of Isaiah, of Job, of Ezekiel—look away, as it were, from the twelve memorial stones set by Joshua to commemorate crossing the Jordan through magic and achieve, by lifting up their eyes to the stars, the sublime intuition: "Though he slay me, yet will I trust in him."

Admirable as are the martyred apostles from a Christian point of view, the unique contribution of the Bible to human typology is the prophet, of whom Jesus is the last. Bards, mystics, seers, druids, saints, God-intoxicated men we have had in many times and literatures, but none resembles these in their union of simplicity and grandeur. The blind man in the New Testament, being cured, saw men as trees walking; the prophets saw them as deeds done and undone. The prophets speak to kings, to nations, and to humanity as if they were themselves sovereign powers; they advise treaties, break alliances, depose rulers, and excoriate priests. Instinctively we think of them as old men (except in the case of Jesus); and artists from Michelangelo to John La Farge have therefore been justified in picturing them as venerable. Each has his special style, ranging from the thick, tenebrous utterances of Jeremiah to the sad serenity of the "Suffering Servant" passages in Isaiah. Apart from the others, the style of Jesus, even across the screen of four biographical accounts, is distinguished for terseness and elegance; in it figure is always controlled, as figure is not controlled in his predecessors. In certain books, the Old Testament prophets exhibit a kind of hallucinatory power—Nahum and Ezekiel are instances. No one can forget the vision of the whirlwind with which Ezekiel opens, nor the nightmare of destruction it is the purpose of the three short chapters of Nahum to depict.

But though the prophets have their distinguishable styles, in the Old Testament they seem, if one reads them continuously, to create an atmosphere, to live in a universe of their own making, out of which a common language springs. It is true that this universe is lively with familiar images—chariots and men of war, grass that comes up and is cut down, fine linen, swords, wine, oil, corn, birds, wind, great beasts, stars, storm, and darkness, but these images are not so much the products of empirical observation as of inwardness, a brooding imagination that overcomes the visible world and sees men and events in it as moving hieroglyphs of an arcane language known or half-known to the elect only. I have spoken of the hallucinatory power of this style. I can illustrate it, I hope, by even so short a passage as this from the second chapter of Nahum:

> But Nineveh is of old like a pool of water; yet they shall flee away. Stand, stand, shall they cry; but none shall look back. Take ye the spoil of silver, take the spoil of gold; for there is none end of the store and glory out of all the pleasant furniture. She is empty, and void, and waste; and the heart melteth, and the knees smite together, and much pain is in all loins, and the faces of them all gather blackness.

As in William Blake, so in this passage: the hypnosis of vision is greater than the sum of its parts and manufactures meaning in proportion as it is extended. Not only does vision appeal to our eschatological sense, which delights in any picture of Götterdämmerung, but the images in such a passage are of the stream-of-consciousness kind. Thus the prophetical books anticipate and often surpass much modern poetry. For example, Conrad Aiken and T. S. Eliot, heaping up disparate, yet associated images in poems like *Senlin* or *The Waste-Land,* consciously or not parallel and repeat the method of the prophets.

Powerful as are the utterances of these men, we know little about them as persons. In one case, Malachi, the book is apparently pseudonymous or anonymous; in other cases, whether the works be short as in the instance of Joel or lengthy as is Isaiah, we apparently have two or more writers cloaking themselves with a single name and speaking, so to say, through a *persona.* Theirs is the power of phantom personalities, and a kind of phantom quality, vague yet powerful, pervades the biblical presentation of personages, with, of course, those brilliant and remarkable exceptions like Jesus, Solomon, Moses, Saul, Peter, and Paul that have stamped themselves upon the imagination of mankind. The Bible names hundreds of human beings; yet the chapters that solemnly trace a genealogy of names that come awkwardly to our English tongues are virtually a satire on immortality. Scarcely less pale are the innumerable kings, who are invariably wicked or good like princes in fairy tales and who, if they are wicked, monotonously repeat the same familiar crimes. None but specialists can care greatly about Jehoram, Joram, Ahaziah, Jehoash, Amaziah, Jehoahaz, and other petty monarchs in II Kings, contemporaries of Elisha. Other names exist as referents for proverbial sayings or tag phrases, such as Agag, who came delicately, thinking the bitterness of death was past; Methuselah, who was very old; Jeshurun, who waxed fat and kicked, or Ananias and Sapphira, who died of lying. Still others exist for a single episode, as Jael, Deborah, Miriam—I choose my illustrations from that minority of biblical personages, the women. The biblical world is overwhelmingly male.

The multitudinous population of this vast collection falls into two principal and unequal divisions: a vast number of persons known as names only or for fable, parable, anecdote, or illustration; and a smaller fraction composed of figures who are memorable as the figures in Homer and Greek tragedy are memorable. The foremost tragic heroes of the Bible are two: Jesus, the most complex character in the whole, the most richly seen, the most fully presented; and, at a great distance from him, Saul.* I say that Jesus is the most richly and fully presented. We see him in every possible light. We have more of his conversation than we have of any other biblical character, not excluding Moses, we see him in his effects upon others, we see him revealed in innumerable episodes, we have all kinds of comment upon him, those of John, Peter, and Pilate springing immediately to mind, and we have him in all sorts of crosslights—confronting crowds as when, on a mountain, he delivers his brilliant and revelatory sermon, alone at Gethsemane, in families, as at the house of Mary, with single interlocutors, as in the case of the rich young ruler, uttering denunciation, speech, and parable (the last a literary form that is virtually a biblical invention), and after his death still power-

* That is, Saul, son of Kish, father of Jonathan, and first king of the ancient Hebrews; not Saul of Tarsus. I think Browning saw this fact when in his poem on Saul he contrasts the Saul "ye remember in glory" with the Saul whose broad brow had been bent from communing with men.

ful, as on the walk to Emmaus and the road to Damascus. The art with which his narrative is made to culminate in the crucifixion scene is triumphant—the necessary labors of scholars at problems of source and text and attribution and style cannot destroy it, just as philologists cannot injure the greatness of Homer, Aeschylus, Sophocles, and Euripides. All questions of theology aside, the presentation of the personality of Jesus is the greatest literary triumph of the ancient world.

In the Bible, character is commonly given and does not develop or exfoliate as it does in Shakespeare or the Greeks. We know Jacob, Esau, Sampson, Abraham, Solomon, Joshua, Ruth, and others immediately, as they are introduced to us, and we grasp at once the strong, simple lines of their characters, usually shaped by ethical presuppositions. The exceptions, like Saul, David, Peter, and Moses, are among the most interesting personages in the book. It is curious that of the apostles only Peter is developed into three-dimensional form, just as among the rulers of Israel only Saul and David are thus developed. Usually the biblical figure, impressive though he may be, is linear, not in the round. If we compare women in the Bible with Helen, Andromache, Clytemnestra, and Electra, we must, I think, concede the superiority of the Greeks in the dynamics of character portrayal. The reason is clear: the writers of the Bible were not, Jesus aside, essentially interested in persons, but in ethics, and the ethical equation is, if I may say so, linear, not geometrical as figure. Biblical personages do not speak in idiosyncratic terms as Homer's people do; they speak, in the main, for moral ends. Exceptions, of course, will occur to every one, but consider the conversations of Pharaoh with Moses and Aaron. His speech is without individual flavor because, since we know that God hardened his heart, he can speak only as an automaton. We do not overhear his speech to understand his psychology as in the case of Achilles or Odysseus; his utterances are simply part of the algebra of a providential situation. In general, I think, the motivation of biblical personages is less interesting than is the case with the Greeks because in most instances what they do is immediately inspired by God or, negatively, God-defying, and therefore they do not make their own decisions. Compare in this connection the complex revelations to Œdipus of the wrongs he has done, with the simple parable of the vineyard by which Nathan convinces David that he is the murderer of Uriah. Since we have been previously informed through Nathan that the Lord has promised, "If he commit iniquity, I will chasten him. . . . But my mercy shall not depart away from him, as I took it from Saul," simple repentance serves, and David, twenty verses later, engenders Solomon upon the body of Bath-sheba, Uriah's wife. The agonized search for meaning and for reconciliation that distinguishes *Œdipus Rex* and informs *Œdipus at Colonnos* can have no part in this frame of reference.

I said early that the great, the incomparable power of the Bible is the power of style. This style is not always equal to the task imposed upon it, and the great failure of the King James version is the Pauline epistles, which are, I infer by reason of their too faithful approach to the originals, often unintelligible. This style has perhaps other weaknesses: the vague sensualism of The Song of Songs never condenses into specificity as the erotic epigrams of the Greek Anthology condense into specific persons, places, times, and emotions. It is also true that the King James Bible cannot avoid the repetitive and the monotonous, which are again, I am sure, qualities of the originals. Finally, in this connection, it is in a sense falla-

158

cious to speak of a single style, since in the Old Testament we run from the simplicity of the opening of Genesis to the thick and crowded pages of Chronicles, and in the New from the clarity of the parables to the metaphysics of John and Paul. But all this is as nothing compared to the total force of this achievement. I do not think it is religion alone, I think it is matchless shaping verbal competence that has turned phrase upon phrase out of the King James Bible into our general speech. "Arose as one man," "the apple of his eye," "busy here and there," "clearer than noonday," "the cattle on a thousand hills," "blossom like a rose," "thorn in the flesh"—how many who speak these familiar phrases are aware that they are found in the 1611 translation? The flexibility of language that in a single book could give us the twenty-third psalm and the angels of Revelations, the story of David and Jonathan and the Plotinian metaphysics of the opening of John, the cosmic vision of Job and the idyll of the book of Ruth is among the wonders of our tongue. Biblical style is a unique creation. It can be parodied but it cannot be paralleled, and, save for revised versions of itself, the Bible, like Shakespeare, is so masterly that no book like it has ever been produced, and in all probability none ever will be. For the only time in English literature, a group of men working together produced a masterpiece, "that inestimable treasure," as they said, "which excelleth all the riches of the earth."

THE NATURE OF LITERARY
HISTORY

Wᴇ ᴀʟʟ think well of literature, which we tend to
define in high and noble terms. Phrases like "the breath
and finer spirit of all knowledge" abound for parts of it,
and we cannot forget that all higher education was once
defined as literature. Thus the educational fund of the
state of Michigan is to this day known as the Literary
Fund, a phrase that points to the time when school and
college curricula were thought of in terms of the printed
and written word, science getting under the main tent as
"natural philosophy," which in turn was a branch of
literary learning we call philosophy. Thus also the humanities, an ambiguous noun many still confuse with the
humane societies or with humanitarian enterprise, descend to us from the *litterae humaniores* of Renaissance
and medieval theorists. Perhaps all this comes to us from
an ancient and sacred concept. "In the beginning was the
Word," according to St. John; and the concept of some
secret power in the Word is not only the heart of the

This address was delivered at Cornell University in July, 1966,
and was printed in the *Journal of the History of Ideas*, April–June,
1967.

mystic vision of the Evangelist but it reappears later in
Faust, that central nineteenth-century creation, in the
scene where the magician-scholar tries to determine
whether the Word, or the Deed, or some other potent
force was the primitive creative power. If Spengler is
right in defining the modern spirit as that of Faustian
man, it is significant that he chose a literary symbol for
this concept rather than a psychiatric, an anthropological,
or a religious one. And although we are living in a period
in which there is a general flight from the word, a period
in which words are no longer as trustworthy as once they
were, becoming propaganda, or double talk, or advertising, a period in which scholarly and conventional English is beneath the dignity of adolescent attention, the
Word has still some power and has not yet wholly given
way to the pictorial arts—billboards that ruin scenery,
television that ruins conversation, visual aids that are
ruining education in the classical sense, and those simplified cartoons on breakfast packages and home appliances
that are one of the causes and one of the consequences of
why Johnny can't read.

American scholarship in all its branches is now probably the best and most various in all the world. We are not
now committed to our former chauvinism, despite American studies programs at home and American Information Libraries abroad. Of course, humanists are unhappy.
As Mr. Trinkaus' interesting study, ironically entitled
Nature's Noblemen, has amply demonstrated, humanists
have been unhappy since they were first invented. Un-
happiness is their characteristic professional disease. Now
as then, they beat their breasts in public, lamenting the
enthusiasm of universities for atom smashers and psychiatric counseling. The great foundations, those unique
American enterprises that neither the New Testament

161

nor the nineteenth century ever imagined, seem more likely to endow investigations in the behavioral sciences than investigations into Etruscan culture or the rhymed Latin poetry of the Middle Ages; and, given a choice between a study of the incidence of non-voting in some Southern commonwealth and a study of the incidence of non-conformity among romantic poets, they will almost invariably choose Alabama over Percy Bysshe Shelley. It is also statistically true that the national budget has for some years been heavily weighted in the direction of the exact sciences rather than of the humanities; and though the Library of Congress is one of the great libraries of the world, the millions of books on its shelves are not all humanistic, and the National Museum of Arts, one of the great museums of the earth, carries on no program quite as highbrow as that of the Warburg Institute in art history and aesthetics. Indeed, the National Science Foundation preceded by some decades the creation of the National Humanities Foundation, two successive directors of which have assured Congress that they will not spend money on anything that is not relevant to current social needs. Perhaps the humanists do lag behind. They suffer from universal approbation, something almost as disastrous as universal disapprobation. The literary scholar has, then, a case.

But the case is an ambiguous one. Literary studies were in a sense never more widely pursued than now. Children in the schools and young persons in the colleges enroll in literary courses, compulsory or otherwise, to an extent not true of other sorts of courses, not even physics, modern psychology, the anthropological study of initiation ceremonies, or coming of age in Samoa. The Modern Language Association of America has in three-quarters of a century risen from a total of about 100 members to a total of more than 22,000, all of whom are interested in language or literature or both, sixty percent of whom are interested in the English language and in literature in English. American literature, which I described some years ago as the orphan child of the curriculum, has matured and given birth to an organization known as the American Studies Association which spreads like the fabulous upas tree until, under the doctrine of relevance, it sometimes threatens the integrity of the old-line English department. I shudder to estimate the membership of the National Council of Teachers of English; but if my memory is right, two years ago it was in the neighborhood of 60,000 teachers, all of them dedicated to the Word. And these principal organizations have generated, or are accompanied by, lesser associated groups, running from the Bibliographical Society of America through the American Association of Research Libraries down to the Melville Society and others dedicated to the highly specialized pursuit of lore about a single name. I am tempted to include here the Baker Street Irregulars which, begun in a spirit of spoofing, has now, as it were, settled down to developing highly specialized and secret lore about Sherlock Holmes and Dr. Watson.

But a change has come over the spirit of the Word. It is no longer ancient and powerful, but contemporary and anxious. Majoring in English in our colleges used to imply some elementary command of literary history. The doctor's degree once meant that the candidate had traveled down the line from Beowulf to Browning, stopping off regularly at intermediate stations like the Elizabethan Age and the Age of Pope, to be inspected by guardians of these successive depots and having his ticket validated by every historical customs officer on the road. Descending at some one of these stations, he stayed for a longer time, coming back to the train with a sound dissertation on "Verbs of Eating and Drinking in Old High Germanic" or "The Use of Doors in the Greek Theater," two dissertations that actually exist and that I have read with proper awe. At the end of his journey which was, somewhat timorously, in the frontier neighborhood of Stevenson and Thomas Hardy, he was given a hood and a diploma, the usual uniform of the literary railroad, and promptly sought employment by the company somewhere along the track.

So far as I can make any sense out of the contemporary anarchy that seems to reign in the kingdom of the Word, much of this journey is now regarded as old hat. The high school pupil studies a book like *Adventures in American Literature,* in which social relevance and picturesqueness are more powerful than the literary classics and a sense of history; and the college senior may graduate *magna cum laude* with a concentration in the English department as innocent of historical implications as modern psychiatric analysis, which it sometimes curiously parallels. Courses in creative writing (recreative would perhaps be a better term), courses in play production, courses in managing a television station, courses in recent poets, courses in modern fiction that include Henry Miller, however they may glide over the contemporary vogue of *Fanny Hill,* courses in the semantics of American English, courses in transformational grammar, courses in oral English, courses in Emily Dickinson, William Faulkner and Melville as symbolic interpreters of *Angst,* alienation, and the artistic desert in which the writer lives (or has lived)—all these can be taken towards a major in the B.A. degree program. If my language seems extreme, the complaint is not mine but extracted from the combined wails of the deans of two

leading law schools, Harvard and Yale, who have pub-
licly denounced current instruction available to future
candidates for a degree in law, on the ground that it
teaches no discipline, inculcates no competency of style,
creates no historical sense, and offers no body of literary
classics common to all educated men.

The enormous increase in literary instruction obviously results from an enormous demand. The means of
satisfying that demand have radically altered from, let us
say, the notion of literary study prevalent in 1910. English
scholars do not ignore the past; if they did the Modern
Language Association would not exist, but they often
tend to interpret the past mainly or wholly in terms of
present taste. Vogue authors, for example, include Henry
James, D. H. Lawrence, T. S. Eliot, John Donne, Dr.
Johnson (who appears somewhat strangely in this cate-
gory), the Brontes, Melville, Thoreau, and in the case of
the greatest of all literary names, the bitter plays of
Shakespeare—*Lear, Measure for Measure, Troilus and
Cressida*—but not the more serene *As You Like It, The
Tempest,* or *Twelfth Night.* We are all for the blasted
heath, the Fool, and the old mad King, but not for the
Forest of Arden, where you shall see no enemy but winter and rough weather. Even Charles Dickens, who used
to be humorous, is now torn between the two Scrooges;
even Mark Twain, who once wrote amusing adventure
stories about Tom Sawyer and his ragged companion, has
been compelled to develop a Tragic Sense, and *Huckleberry Finn,* formerly a picaresque romance, has been
revamped into an image of a deep-seated and ineradicable
conflict between light and blackness in the American
psyche.

In one sense all this is nothing novel, nothing strange.
We have had vogue authors before. To the generation of

Byron, Torquato Tasso was a great modern spirit, not because he wrote a Christian epic about the conquest of Jerusalem but because he was unjustly imprisoned by a tyrannical ducal family who declared him mad since he had fallen in love with a young woman of the reigning house. The age of Bacon cited with relish authors in Greek and Latin we are no longer capable of reading except in translation. They found some great emotional satisfaction in passages from Aulus Gellius or Plotinus that leave us gasping as we hunt up the footnotes. I doubt that Plutarch's *Lives* have the significance for contemporary Americans they had for William Shakespeare; I think few of us study Boethius for consolation and pleasure as Chaucer seems to have done; and such modern fiction as I have read dealing with Arthurian romance, which it usually burlesques, does not solemnly cite Nennius, or Wace, or Geoffrey of Monmouth to authenticate the personages and events of the story or assure the reader that here is history *wie es eigentlich gewesen.*

All this does not mean that historical studies in literature are not today pursued. The annual bibliography of *PMLA,* which used to be a modest annex to that respectable journal, today requires a set of special committees to prepare it, and a special supplementary issue of the magazine to print it. It runs every year to thousands of items historically classified by language, country, and epoch. In the hiring halls of the universities or at annual meetings of *MLA* the formula is still to find a promising young specialist in the eighteenth century or the middle ages, a Shakespeare man or a Henry James man, or one of those rarer birds, a specialist in Old English Literature or in the literature of colonial America. At annual meetings of *MLA* or of the regional societies associated with it, at annual sessions of the English Institute, the Renaissance

166

Society, or the Medieval Academy of America research papers are produced, often of weight and insight, the majority of them within the context of some historical framework, whether they deal with a new source for Poe's "The Fall of the House of Usher" or a "Reinterpretation of the Christian and Virgilian Elements in *Beowulf*."

I have said that American scholarship is now possibly the best in the world, in the sense that our bibliographical resources, the organization of our libraries, the plenitude of our research articles, the generosity of our university presses in publishing learned books, the policies of academic administrators in giving grants-in-aid, reduced teaching hours, and leaves of absence (sabbatical or otherwise), and in making post-doctoral fellowships available for work in libraries and collections here and abroad are among the great triumphs of the history of the human mind. Much of this activity is of course conducted on the brick theory of learning; that is, I manufacture and bring a brick to some mysterious central site, where someone else even more mysterious is going to erect the fair cathedral of total historical scholarship. I have somewhere read there is in Empedocles a pedant who, desiring to sell his house, carried about with him a brick as a sample to show prospective purchasers. The charge has been brought against our scholarly bricks that they are atomistic, too many in number, and too small for domestic use. Yet even these reveal a genuine commitment to historical scholarship.

In the classroom, however, we are slightly apologetic about being literary historians; that is, scholars in the philosophic sense. Vast forces of opinion, both popular and educational, are organized against specialism, which, it seems, is forever narrow; against pedantry, which has been defined as somebody else's scholarship; against the dead weight of the past, the past being in this context irrelevant until we transform it through the enchantment of criticism, the witchcraft of psychiatric analysis, or the sympathetic magic of totem and tabu in writers who never heard these terms, into an anticipatory mirror-image of the present. The general theory of Hamlet's contemporaneousness is, it seems, wholly right: "the times are out of joint—O cursed spite! that we were ever born to set them right"—witness the transformation of Dickens into ego-projection, the dismissal of "The Elegy in a Country Churchyard" as irrelevant to a nation that has invented the funeral home, and the conferring of full American citizenship upon Sigmund Freud and Carl Jung. Writers like Carlyle and Ruskin are, in comparison, out of date because they are irrelevant to Kafka and Kierkegaard, social alienation, and the lack of beauty in an industrial culture. Their exclusion is somewhat astonishing inasmuch as the great central chapters of *Sartor Resartus* deal with the Everlasting Nay, the Center of Indifference, and the Everlasting Yea, thus anticipating the doctrine of modern *Angst;* and the denunciation by John Ruskin of man's spoilage of the landscape through industrial greed anticipates by almost a hundred years Lady Bird Johnson's plea to rid the countryside of automobile graveyards and to restore beauty to America.

We have, then, an immense historical scholarship, but I suggest we have engendered through our literary studies only a minor historical sense or sensitivity, call it which you will. Yet in these same seventy-five years we have had the sweeping historical surveys of Wells and Spengler, Toynbee's vast attempt at a total history of all the cultures that ever were or ever will be, and a rich library of books about historical theory by scholars like

R. G. Collingwood, Maurice Mandelbaum, and a dozen others. We restore literary shrines like the Alcott homestead in Concord or the Mark Twain mansion in Hartford. We go to immense pains to collect what we can of Egyptian, Babylonian, Pompeian, Medieval, Chinese, Japanese, and early African art, partly because of its beauty, partly because it stimulates modern artists, partly because from it we can partially reconstruct the life and times of civilizations far away or long ago; and we endeavor to exhibit these fragments of early ages not as isolated objects but in relation to other artifacts of their own times, as when we put together a Roman atrium or a medieval chapel, or preserve or imitate early Plymouth, colonial Williamsburg, or the territorial capital of Montana. We seem eager to know how these peoples lived and loved and died; how they worshipped; how they felt and what they felt about; what costumes they wore, what cups they drank from, what gods they adored, how they killed their enemies or enslaved them.

But we seem a little chary of going at literary history in quite this vivid way, though of course one cannot present the history of poetry as one can, like Sir Arthur Evans, reconstruct (however questionably) a Cretan palace at Knossos. Yet the value systems of these vanished epochs are, if they are anywhere registered, as sensitively registered in literature as they are in the images of the gods, or the hairpins and bracelets of fashionable Roman women upon which we gaze with fascination in art museums and classical collections. It is ironical that the literary remains of vanished cultures are in truth one of the principal criteria of these collections, these meticulous restorations of rooms, houses, and villas, and these pictorial reconstructions of generations past.

And here I must particularize. We restore the text of

Catullus or Nathaniel Hawthorne with the greatest care, just as we paste together the shattered amphorae found in our archeological excavations. But the restoration of the texts of Catullus or Hawthorne or a hundred other authors, taken atomistically as jobs that end in themselves, is not literary history, it is only preparing for literary history. Literary history requires a certain imaginative reconstruction and empathetic insight. It is as if, having pieced together a statue of the Mexican war-god in one place, and reconstructed a teocalli or sacrificial pyramid in another, and found and cleaned some stone adzes in a third locality, we should lack the curiosity to find out whether these three objects, so meticulously handled, had any conceivable relation among themselves.

If literary history as a major cultural enterprise is at a discount among us, it is easy to understand and sympathize with some of the reasons for this general disinclination to pursue the subject on a grand scale. In the first place, most of the literary histories we have had—and I confine myself to histories of English and American literature for simplicity, though I have some reason to suppose that like weaknesses appear in the histories of other literatures—are not in most cases enchanting. These literary histories fall into certain easily distinguishable classes. The most naive among them, or rather the most naive treatment of literary history, is probably that of the political and social historians, who in narrating the history of some epoch—an easy example is found in *The Rise of American Civilization* by Charles and Mary Beard—conscientiously include literature as a sub-topic, just as they conscientiously include other sub-topics like the rise of athletic sports or the growth of journalism, and produce as a kind of appendix to a really lively discussion of American life a sort of handbook of works and authors that has been simplified and reduced from some larger handbook. A catalogue of American railroad companies with occasional comments upon their principal trains would do about as well for a treatment of the transportation problem in the United States. I am somehow reminded of the classic discussion of the author of *Moby-Dick* in Barrett Wendell's *Literary History of America,* where we read that Herman Melville never came to fruition.

Historians do not pretend to either aesthetic or critical sensitivity, nor do they have a professional education in either world literature or the literature of the English-speaking peoples. Consequently, they are forced to borrow; and many traditional types of literary history from which they borrow are of the encyclopedia or dictionary order. From Bishop Bale's *Illustrium Majoris Britanniae Scriptorum Summarium,* which was put together in the mid-sixteenth century, through Henry Hallam's *Introduction to the Literature of Europe in the Fifteenth, Sixteenth and Seventeenth Centuries,* published between 1837 and 1839, down to the latest Barnes and Noble *Outline of English Literature* for a quick cram session, the handbook-dictionary-encyclopedia pattern prevails. One goes back to Bale as a source book; one consults Hallam because, dull and accurate, he is the handiest author to consult; one uses the Barnes and Noble outline or any other paper-back outline-chronicle as one would use any reference work, of which we have dozens in most libraries. They give the facts, or purport to; minor errors about dates and editions can be corrected if necessary. Yet if, following Pater, we inquire in whom the stir, the life of a period shows itself, these compendia will never tell us. They resemble the registers of churches; they represent a principle of orderly entombment, whereas what we are looking for is the same sense that we get from the period rooms in a museum, the Emily Dickinson room in the Houghton Library, or the Mark Twain house in Hartford—a sense of the life, the culture, the color, the movement of an earlier age.

There is a second type of literary history, far more readable though often perverse and wrong-headed. But its pages at least leave you with an impression that the author has not lived among the zombies, that he has meditated on the lives and passions of men and on the place of literature in human activity. These books set out to find, or begin by assuming, that there is some single and uniform principle, some central law in literary development which, being discovered, both unifies and illuminates a national literature. The great classical example is Taine's *History of English Literature,* published in Paris between 1856 and 1865 and promptly translated into English. Taine at one time had enormous vogue both among literary scholars and among social historians, and his way of writing influenced such men as Moses Coit Tyler, who finished at Cornell what he had begun at Michigan, a history of literature in America from 1607 to 1783, in a total of four volumes published from 1878 and 1897, and still not superseded as a chronicle of colonial and revolutionary writing in the future United States. A child of advanced thought in the nineteenth century, Taine sought for some general sociological and moral law; and his explanation of the ultimate characteristics of any national literature is simple and sweeping: *le milieu, la race, le moment.* That is to say, if you would seek the secret of literary development, study the environment, the racial characteristics, and the historical epochs in which literature has been produced. Here is at least an organizational principle superior to the dreary annalistic approach of

Hallam or Bishop Bale; and here are some great half-truths if they are not whole truths. Environment *does* matter: if Beethoven had been born in Arabia, would he have been the self-tormenting genius we know about? Race also matters: The whole Anglo-Saxon tradition lies behind *Henry V*. If Wordsworth had been born an Indian on the upper Amazon, do you think—I borrow from Aldous Huxley—we would have had anything like Tintern Abbey or the hint that Lucy was

> A violet by a mossy stone
> Half hidden from the eye!
> —Fair as a star, when only one
> Is shining in the sky?

And time and circumstance matter also. I find it hard to imagine *Alice in Wonderland*'s being written by a contemporary of the Latin historian Orosius, who thought and taught in the 5th century that the world was going to end in the year 1000, and who was translated into Old English by that most serious of monarchs, Alfred the Great. It is only when you come down to cases that Taine becomes ridiculous, as when he infers that the marshlands of Anglo-Saxon England affected poetry and that the thick English style of Dickens' novels owes something to London fogs. Taine is nevertheless important because he moves in the right direction, he sets our feet in the way that they perhaps ought to go. But obviously he is simplicistic. He makes us think of his great contemporary, Herbert Spencer, who brought all science, all philosophy, all art, and all theology under a single law, that of evolution and dissolution, the phrasing of which strikes us nowadays as impossible. The Law of Evolution, he wrote, is "an integration of matter and concomitant dissipation of motion, during which the matter passes from an indefinite incoherent homogeneity to a definite coherent heterogeneity, and during which the retained motion undergoes a parallel transformation." If this or something like it, emphasizing the principle of the universal dissipation of energy, comforted Henry Adams, it comforted almost nobody else; and no literary historian has ever successfully established the evolution and dissolution of literary types under Spencer's law of evolution and dissolution.

There have been other reductions of literary history to a single naïve principle. Thus Marxist history tends in this direction. Books like the late Ludwig Lewisohn's *Expression in the United States* substitute for the Taine formula a concept that Dionysus should replace Apollo as the god of our idolatry, and set up a doctrine of repression and escape. Vernon L. Parrington wrote his influential three-volume interpretation of American thought in literary form as a conflict of Ormuz and Ahrimanes. The good guys were the liberals, the bad guys were the conservatives, and writers who refused to take sides were consigned to a kind of aesthetic limbo. Latterly we have varied this simplicity by employing the unconscious as our unifying principle. The unconscious appears, not surprisingly, unconsciously; and standard classics are now transmogrified into a weird dance of symbols that obfuscate what seems to most readers and older scholars the plain meaning of the text.

A camel was once defined as a horse put together by a committee; and the third main type of literary history is the committee-written work. The antecedent of this is, I think, in political history; after the success of the Cambridge histories of the ancient world, medieval times, the modern world, and so on, works to which individual specialists contributed particular chapters, usually heavy-handed, it was inevitable that the same formula should be applied to literary history. The first notable product of the camel method was the *Cambridge History of English Literature,* which began publication in 1907 and ran to 14 volumes. To these a fifteenth was by and by added. Individual chapters were often brilliant, but the work as a whole was dark with excess of light. Nor did the method improve when this was followed by the *Cambridge History of American Literature* in four volumes published as three. Each chapter had attached to it (in the rear of the volumes) a bibliography, but the bibliographies varied in extensiveness and accuracy. Above all, the difficulty was the lack of any unified point of view; this was literary history seen through a kaleidoscope. So much dissatisfaction was expressed with this history that specialists resolved to try it all over again. The result was *The Literary History of the United States* in three volumes, the third consisting of one of the most awkwardly arranged bibliographies of modern times. The work has been reprinted several times, occasionally revised, and now carries with it an additional small volume supplementing the bibliographical learning of the first edition. *The Literary History of the United States* is better organized than its predecessor; it is divided into periods, each beginning with a chapter or two of social history and a discussion of modes of publishing. But this mechanical pattern does not guarantee uniformity of treatment in the following chapters. This work, which everybody in American literature owns, still remains a camel. There are of course other volumes written in collaboration, such as the *Literary History of England* by Messrs. Baugh, Brooke, Chew, Malone, and Sherburn, and since the committee was in that case smaller, they brought to it something nearer a uniform system of interpretation. And there are histories of literature in a series of smaller books, each by an individual scholar, single units of which have value and insight. But these are commonly got out for textbook purposes. Textbook publishers, like weather vanes, veer with the slightest wind that blows; they register not so much a concern for aesthetics and philosophy as a profound belief that any majority of potential purchasers want what they want when they want it. In the textbook world as in the department store, the customer is always right.

What, then, should a great literary history be? I begin by insisting that any great history of an art should itself be a work of art. All great political histories are works of art—Thucydides, Gibbon, Parkman, Greene's *History of the English People,* Henry Adams' *History of the United States during the Administrations of Jefferson and Madison* are examples. John Addington Symonds' volumes on the Italian Renaissance are analogues in cultural history. George Sarton's *History of Science,* so far as it went before his death, is a parallel in the world of scientific ideas; Chandler Post's *History of Spanish Painting,* and Moses Coit Tyler's *History of American Literature during the Colonial Time* and his *Literary History of the American Revolution* are exemplars among the arts.

When I call these standard titles works of art in themselves, however outmoded we may think this or that passage in them and however we may wish to correct this or that judgment or conclusion, I refer to at least three qualities. The first is personal involvement: the writer has historical imagination, empathy, and a profound belief that the subject has vast meaning for human culture. Thus Gibbon felt that the decline and fall of the Roman Empire was a matter of fundamental importance to the modern world. Symonds was committed to the assumption that getting the human race, or at least Western man, out from under the shadow of the Middle Ages into the sunlight of the Renaissance was a great step forward in the life of humanity. George Sarton in his preface declares that he is discussing the whole of ancient science because ancient science was a part of ancient culture and wisdom, something the contemporary world does not dare to lose; the book, he says, "tries to show the growth of the human spirit in its natural background." Moses Coit Tyler, writing the history of American literature from 1607 to 1783, feels that he is at the very source and root of the American idea and is passionately concerned that his readers shall understand not merely the facts but the implications of history. Probably great history is always written with some sort of bias; certainly it cannot be written without a deep sense of personal involvement; and most emphatically, it is not the product of impersonality, of objectivity, of that curious fear of professional contradiction which is the bane of literary scholarship.

In the second place, these histories rest upon a long acquaintance and living with the subject. The writers are steeped in information, they live backward, they are themselves imaginatively involved, they are participants in the disastrous expedition to Syracuse, or sit in his studio with Velasquez, or struggle with the dark powers of stupidity and sin with Jonathan Edwards at Northampton and Stockbridge. They do not write out of sentimentality, they do not, as the phrase goes, "appreciate" the art of literature or the beauties of science, they do not turn Jefferson's first inaugural into a moral lesson in tolerance and American idealism. They are superior to this naiveté. They are so steeped in knowledge, they have passed beyond particulars into philosophy, they live, as it were, double lives—one in the present tense, and one, intelligent, informed, vital, philosophic, human and sometimes humorous, in that portion of the human story that has claimed and riveted their attention so long, they cannot exist without expressing in orderly prose its greatness and its importance.

In the third place, these works have structure. In the simplest terms they exhibit, even when they are incomplete, an Aristotelian beginning, middle, and end. They are put together as a tragedy or a well-proportioned building is put together. The parts melt into unity, they do not insist on being divisive and anarchical. We know where we are in Gibbon—we begin with the age of the Antonines, when, under a succession of capable rulers, Western man was on the whole happier and better governed than he ever has been before or since, and the rest of the work, the whole six volumes, is a long chronicle of fatal errors ranging from Christian zeal to general massacre. We know where we are in John Addington Symonds: Western man has been too long shrouded in clerical obfuscation, he has by a happy chance stumbled upon a new reading of antiquity, and a rich and powerful individualism follows, which, if it sometimes expresses itself in treachery, blood, and crime, expresses itself also in some of the greatest imaginative works, some of the greatest philosophic inventions that man has ever known.

In the art of great historical writing, whether it concerns politics or music, the aesthetic consideration of the structure of the whole is as important as accuracy of detail, the chapters of the work are more than disparate essays, they are distinguishable elements leading toward unity, and the style is not that of an expert speaking to specialists but that of a man speaking to men—not to school teachers, nor to college departments, nor to museum directors, nor to the keepers of rare books and collections of manuscripts. We have, in sum, in the books I have cited a reading of life—the tragedy of Greece, the downfall of Rome, the strength and anarchism of individualism, the creation of science, the passing on of the torch from painter to painter, the philosophic origins of the modern republic.

If literature be what it purports to be—a great, profound, and imaginative statement of human motives, human experience, human folly, and human wisdom; if it is, indeed, the best thoughts in the best order; if it is the breath and finer spirit of all knowledge; if we are to understand both its development through the centuries and its significance to modern man, we must, when we write its history, distinguish between the necessary technicalities of literary studies and the mode of writing literary history. Literary history, like any other sort of history, should be as accurate as we can make it; and our higher learning is necessarily directed towards perfecting the technology of scholarly research. We must learn our way around libraries—not merely the libraries of today, but those of the past: hence the need of bibliographical lore. We must know enough about individual authors not to confuse the order of their literary development—not to assume, for instance, that *Titus Andronicus* and *The Tempest* were written simultaneously; and if my illustration makes the English faculty smile, do not most of us vaguely assume that all of Plato's dialogues were written, so to speak, by a single timeless mind in a single timeless world? We need to know not merely the order of literary works but the personal experiences that influenced them or called them forth, as, Byron's exile from English society, Chaucer's Italian journey, Henry Adams' response to his wife's suicide, Trollope's attitude toward literary composition, the early poverty of George Bernard Shaw, and the years of neglect into which Herman Melville fell. Hence, biography. We need in the third place to be certain that the literary work is genuine, something neither forged nor tampered with, and we need to understand in their proper original sense the words it uses. Hence the necessity for textual criticism and for appropriate linguistic mastery not merely of the various phases of our English tongue, but of relevant foreign languages, ancient or modern. The continual sharpening and refining of information in areas like these justifies the contributions we make to scholarly journals.

But these contributions are only preparatory and subordinate, like the training program of football players or the practice of scales on the piano—they should be conducted in appropriate private professional contexts, not be mistaken for the ending end, as Sir Philip Sidney would say, of literary history. The fact that the text of most school editions of *The Scarlet Letter* is corrupt is not equivalent to an authoritative statement of the place of that ambiguous writer, Hawthorne, in the development of American culture.

Above all—and this is my final plea—literary history is a problem of culture. Writers partake of the cultural, intellectual, and political movements of their time. They know kings and statesmen, painters and philosophers, musicians and poets, even generals, clergymen, business men, scientists, social workers, and day laborers. They express an age. But an age expresses itself not in poetry only, or the drama, the essay, the novel, and literary criticism. It expresses itself in philosophy, the fine arts, international diplomacy, the movements of armies, city existence and country life. Is there no important analogue between the fugues of Bach and qualities of the closed couplet of Dryden and Pope? Is there no living connection between Matthew Arnold's experience as school

180

inspector and his *Culture and Anarchy?* If Emerson's earlier prose is a statement of what later commentators called the "Newness," are not the radical philosophies current in the age of Jackson, the destruction of the United States Bank, the panics of 1837 and 1857 as relevant to Emerson as the truth that he read Swedenborg and Sampson Reed? Is there no conceivable meaning in the fact that Gilbert and Sullivan, Augustus de Morgan's *Budget of Paradoxes,* publication of the collected works of George Riemann, the non-Euclidean geometer, the earlier paintings of Seurat, and those amusing spoofs, *Flatland* and T. A. Guthrie's *Vice Versa* come along together, all exercises in ingenuity, all denying that any statement of the truth is absolute, all asserting in their several ways that our knowledge of things is relative to the viewpoint of the observer?

If we truly believe that literature expresses the best that has been said and thought in the world in cultural epochs of great importance, we ought to be content in the writing of literary history with nothing less than a total command of the culture which the literature expresses. True, this is literally impossible; but it is a task that historians set themselves every day. No historian interested in antiquity believes for a single moment that he has mastered the total life of Greece and the Roman Empire. But he does not therefore characteristically argue that because specialists in archeology know more than he does about Greek temples, he should ignore Greek architecture. This, however, is the kind of facile evasion into which much literary history falls.

To me it is naive for the specialist in the literature of, say, the English eighteenth century to confess not merely that he knows little about the French *philosophes* and the progress of poetry on the Continent, but also that he has little notion of music from Bach through Mozart to Beethoven, no interest in painting from Sir Peter Lely to William Blake, small concern for dress and costume and manners during the century, only a tepid enthusiasm for the literature of exploration, and small ability to cope with the theory and practice of science in that great age. His business, he claims, is with literature and with literature only. Called upon to deliver a manuscript about English poetry from Dryden to Wordsworth, he delivers one impeccable in scholarship, yet blind to eighteenth-century life. Is it to be inferred that members of Johnson's Club were interested only in books? Were they not concerned about the activities of Sir Joshua Reynolds, the astronomical discoveries of Sir William Herschel, papers read before the Royal Society, Lord Monboddo's astonishing theories about language, orangoutangs and the human race, Blackstone's doctrines of law and government, and the eternal puzzle of the female sex? The most superficial reading of Boswell's Johnson denies the queer assumption that authors live only for publishers and for each other.

I hold, then, that literary history, difficult to write and requiring, if it is to be excellent, the kind of patience that brought Gibbon's *Decline and Fall* into being, should be written as the highest form of cultural history; that though individual volumes in literary history now publishing are often excellent works, we still lack a philosophy of the subject; that literary history requires the spacious thinking about civilization and literature more common among historians than among literary specialists; and that, though our graduate training must still insist upon the elements of scholarship, mature scholarship must in this particular look beyond the monographic concept of research now dominant, towards larger horizons and a richer philosophy about the place of arts in human society.

"MASSACHUSETTS, THERE
SHE IS"

Scholars and historians of ideas are beginning to doubt
the validity of a traditional judgment on the so-called
Golden Day in New England. This judgment can be
summarized in two titles by Van Wyck Brooks: *The
Flowering of New England,* which comes down to 1865,
and *New England: Indian Summer,* which ends at 1915.
In the first book all is bright and forward-looking; the
second exudes a general flavor of mild decay. The first
assumes that the New England mind, by which Brooks
principally means literature, achieved force, maturity,
and unity in the 1850's; the second infers that after 1865
force and unity disintegrated. Other books made a like
assumption. Thus F. O. Matthiessen, who drew most of
his illustrations from New England, devoted his remarkable study, *American Renaissance,* to the 1850's. A year
earlier, however, F. L. Pattee published a study called

Under the title "The Unity of New England Culture" this
paper was read before the Massachusetts Historical Society in 1967
and published in their *Proceedings* in 1968. I have changed the
title, borrowing the phrase from Daniel Webster's "Reply to
Hayne." Webster's phrase is commonly misquoted as "Massachusetts, there she stands."

The Feminine Fifties, which assumed that Hawthorne meant what he said when he talked about a damned mob of scribbling women.

Masterpieces appeared in the fifties, but it is one thing to note masterpieces and another to infer from them a unified culture. Let me examine the inference. In the first place literary historians themselves split this literature into two parts. They differentiate between a Cambridge-Boston group and a transcendentalist or Concord group. The ideal of the first was cultural cosmopolitanism; of the second, individualism that sometimes went to seed as eccentricity. This differentiation has social meaning. Boston was then readier to accept writers like Longfellow and Holmes than it was to accept writers like Thoreau and Emerson. This is evident from some sale figures.* Thus, among subscribers to *The Dial,* principal organ of transcendentalism, Boston furnished only thirty names. Hawthorne's *The Blithedale Romance* virtually ceased to sell when readers discovered it was based on that radical experiment, Brook Farm; and Hawthorne's royalties from *The Scarlet Letter* were only about $450. Yet Susan Warner made $4,500 in six months from *The Wide, Wide World,* and Maria Susanna Cummins of Ipswich in 1854 sold 40,000 copies of *The Lamplighter* in six weeks. Thoreau's *Week on the Concord and Merrimac Rivers* (1849) sold about 200 copies, and the rest were remaindered to the author; and though *Walden* did pretty well in 1859, there was no second edition until some years after Thoreau's death. Because they combined amusement, information, and shock, Melville's books about the cannibals sold, but of *Moby-Dick,* which had only a small printing in 1851, 300 unsold copies remained in 1853 to be

* I add that for five years after 1847 Emerson's *Poems* sold about 300 copies annually, Longfellow's about 2,000 a year.

burned up in a fire that also destroyed the plates. I add parenthetically that the only writers associated with the Golden Day to give the Lowell lectures between 1839 and 1860 were the conservative Oliver Wendell Holmes, and James Russell Lowell, just before he became a Harvard professor.

This suggests that in the fifties New England culture was not at unity with itself. There was considerable tension between mercantile culture and the literary men we now admire, and also within mercantile culture itself. In the fifties Boston was a boom-and-bust town. The Railroad Jubilee of 1851 represented boom; the panic of 1857 represented the bust. The Jubilee lasted three days, involved a parade three and a half miles long, and a pavilion on the Common for 3,600 diners, and commanded the presence of the governor-general of Canada and the president of the United States. That year Elias Hasket Derby, writing in *Hunt's Merchants' Magazine,* prophesied that within twenty-five years assessed property in Boston would be worth a billion and a quarter; all that was needed were peace and a stopping of radical agitation over slavery, popular rights, and religion. But the Jubilee was a speculative, not an economic, triumph; within a year or so, defalcations were uncovered in railroad investments, the stock of one such company fell from 102 to 67, of another from 111 to 52, payments of dividends on about a third of the railroad stocks ceased, and of interest on their funded debts in the same proportion. The panic of 1857 was deeply disturbing. Banks suspended payment, Phillips and Sampson, leading publishers, failed, the father of Charles W. Eliot lost all his money, and the father of Henry Lee Higginson wrote his son that "a whirlwind of terrific power and significance was sweeping over the country." A pamphlet of 1858 by Erastus

Bigelow bitterly reproached investors for their "rash and indiscriminating" stock-buying and their equally unreasonable refusal to invest. In the *Vernon Papers* Edward Everett Hale blamed the whole thing on debt, but the first number of the *Atlantic Monthly* held God responsible, for God "rules the market" and permits economic catastrophe as He permits natural catastrophe. In truth, from the Mexican War, which ended in 1848, to the Civil War, which began in 1861, a sorely tried mercantile group that wanted peace and prosperity exhibits the psychology of a siege.

Sound religion was, they thought, being assailed by radicals. Emerson's "Divinity School Address" of 1838, attacked by Andrews Norton as the latest form of infidelity and at the request of the divinity faculty answered by William Ware, kept Emerson out of the good graces of Harvard until 1866. It could not be forgotten. Its doctrine was reenforced by his essays and lectures and by village philosophers like Thoreau, bluestockings like Margaret Fuller, and dreamers who never met a payroll like Amos Bronson Alcott. Moreover, there was the Catholic problem. In 1854 John S. Orr, costuming himself in a white robe and blowing a trumpet, announced he was divinely appointed to destroy the Catholic Church; a regiment of soldiers had to be alerted against a threatened riot, and the triumph of the Know-Nothing party in the mid-decade meant, among other things, the dissolution of militia companies supposed to be Catholic.

Sound education was also attacked. Harvard was safe enough under the five presidents between Quincy and Eliot who were, as Morison suavely puts it, not really successful. Just before the decade opened, that radical, Horace Mann, issued his famous *Tenth Annual Report*. Francis Wayland, president of Brown, had taught in textbooks widely used that riches are the way God rewards a good Christian; Horace Mann, however, not only wanted the rich to educate the poor but also declared that no man has any title to wealth and that if the wealthy did not accept the school tax, they would be embezzling from children.

There was radicalism wherever you looked. I pass over such famous names and events as Garrison, John Brown, the Dred Scott decision, the Anthony Burns riot; I note only that most literary men were on the side of the agitators. Even Longfellow, Smith Professor of Romance Languages at Harvard, had earlier published a little abolitionist collection, *Poems on Slavery*. Emerson wrote of the Fugitive Slave Act that the law was a filthy enactment and by God, he would not obey it. We think of Whittier as a fading good gray Quaker poet; we forget that he was as vituperative about the South, where New England bought cotton and sold goods, as the South was about New England. Daniel Webster opposed abolitionist violence and strove to preserve the Union; the sober *Dictionary of American Biography* notes that he was the special advocate of the new industrial interests; and of Webster Emerson bitterly said in 1850: "The word liberty in the mouth of Mr. Webster sounds like the word love in the mouth of a courtesan." Emerson continued to lecture in Boston, but whereas he had earlier got $57 on an average for a lecture, in the mid-fifties he was getting only $40. In 1850 he wrote that after speaking and writing for twenty-five years, he had not one disciple—an exaggeration that is illuminating. Obviously business leaders and literary men did not see eye to eye.

We who read these authors as classics do not realize the State Street distrust of literary radicalism, nor the vehemence of the literary response. Of the years from

1790 to 1820 Emerson wrote in 1852 that there was not a book, a speech, a conversation, or a thought in the state; the important thing is not the exaggeration but the attitude. "Stand in State Street," he urged, "and see the heads and the gait and gestures of the men; they are doomed ghosts going under judgment all day long." "Boston or Brattle Street Christianity," he said, "is a compound of forces, or the best diagonal line that can be drawn between Jesus Christ and Abbot Lawrence." "The lesson of these days," he wrote in 1854, "is the vulgarity of wealth." "The view of Transcendentalism in State Street," he declared, "is that it threatens to invalidate contracts." Addressing the Mechanics' Apprentices' Library Association, he told them: "The young man on entering life, finds the way to lucrative employments blocked with abuses. The ways of trade are grown selfish to the borders of theft, and supple to the borders (if not beyond the borders) of fraud." Thoreau defined an American as one "who ventures to live only by the aid of the Mutual Insurance Company, which has promised to bury him decently." If one examines the first chapter of *Walden* carefully, he discovers it is a parody of an annual business report, an attack on money-getting, and a satire on economic theory. Respectability was not amused by these and other assaults. There is usually a war of the members between the business world and the writing world, but the antagonism in New England in the fifties seems to me so bitter as to preclude any theories about a unified culture.

A great unifying force appeared, of course—the Civil War. There were fraud and corruption in New England as elsewhere, there was an anti-draft riot in Boston, not, however, so ghastly as that in New York, there were many who wanted peace at any price, and those who couldn't stand Abraham Lincoln. But a study of the Boston *Transcript* from 1861 to 1865 will reveal an extraordinary degree of commitment. New England wrath was aroused by the assault on the Sixth Massachusetts in 1861 in Baltimore and by the discourteous treatment of the body of Colonel Robert Gould Shaw after the bloody failure at Fort Wagner in 1863. Victory now justified the protest of the abolitionists against slavery and the indignation of the conservatives against disunion; it fused and validated a New England point of view, nobly expressed by Lowell in the great "Commemoration Ode" of 1865. That Vermont suffered the highest number of casualties in proportion to its population of any state on either side, and that a Vermont brigade endured greater losses than any other brigade from a single state in the North show how deeply New England was involved. Tensions between the muse and the marketplace did not of course vanish between 1861 and 1915; I believe, however, that postbellum New England culture acquired a dynamism and a unity undervalued by historians.

Before turning to this matter, may I dispose of a few fallacies? One is that as New York became the chief publishing center of the country, the intellectual dynamism of the Boston area therefore declined. This is a *non sequitur,* and it seemed so to Thomas Bailey Aldrich, who dryly observed that whenever an author died in Boston, the New Yorkers thought they had a literary center. Authors do not necessarily live in publishing centers. The machinery of publishing today is centered in New York; authorial typewriters, however, can be heard on Cape Cod or Martha's Vineyard, in Cambridge or Connecticut, far away from the linotype machines and the advertising agencies.

The second fallacy concerns the diminished force of

New England in the nation. When Webster delivered his Seventh of March speech, there were only sixty senators, of whom New England had twelve; today there are a hundred. In 1850 New England held about a ninth of the population; today, only about one-eighteenth. The seaports of New England have dwindled in importance, the promising New England railways are bad, New England agriculture is a lost cause, and in many fields New England industry has declined in relation to the gross national product. But this is to confuse quantity in one area with quality in another, Rome with Athens. The fact that New York University enrolls something like sixty or seventy thousand students does not therefore argue the inferiority of Yale and Harvard.

A third fallacy imputes a special stuffiness to New England, notably to Boston. The refusal of the trustees of the Boston Public Library to give space to MacMonnies' statue of the "Dancing Bacchante," the activities of the Watch and Ward Society, and illegal censorship by the police are gravely cited as evidence of an intolerable Puritan tradition. What is in question, however, is not Puritanism but middle-class propriety, and a similar indictment could be drawn against all sorts of centers from Philadelphia to Los Angeles. Boston may have been peculiar, but it was not unique. Moreover, everything depends on where you look for suppression. For example, New England produced Benjamin Tucker, the philosophic anarchist, who for years wrote editorials for the Boston *Globe* and simultaneously edited an anarchist periodical called *Liberty;* he also sold *Leaves of Grass* and Tolstoy's *Kreutzer Sonata* in spite of the police. He was succeeded by Stephen T. Byington, a valued proofreader at Ginn and Company, another philosophical anarchist, who translated Max Stirner's *The Ego and His Own* and who in my lifetime was writing highly literate letters of protest to the principal Boston newspapers.

A fourth fallacy is that the *Atlantic Monthly,* regarded as the central expression of the New England mind, has been a parochial magazine. I have gone through its files from 1857 to 1890, and whatever its other defects, parochialism is not one. Every volume contains stories or articles concerning England, France, Germany, Italy, the Scandinavias, or the Orient. Problems of economic and social change, cultural problems, discussions of science and of national policy, contributions by writers like Henry James, articles by a zealous reformer like Edward Atkinson and by a zealous conservative like the elder Henry Cabot Lodge appear. In comparison the *New Yorker* is really provincial.

These things out of the way, it might suffice as comment upon the theory that the New England mind weakened after 1865 to say that a period which saw some or all of the best work of Francis Parkman, William James, George Santayana, William Graham Sumner, Josiah Willard Gibbs, Francis Child, E. A. Robinson, Sarah Orne Jewett, Alice Brown, Mary E. Wilkins Freeman, Charles W. Eliot, Charles Eliot Norton, Francis A. Walker, Edward Bellamy, Benjamin Orange Flower, William Dwight Whitney the philologian, Robert A. Woods the settlement worker, Christopher Columbus Langdell, Winslow Homer, Horatio Parker, Charles Ives, Charles Francis Adams II, Henry Adams, Bliss Perry, Justin Winsor, John Fiske, Frank W. Taussig, Albert Bushnell Hart, Phillips Brooks, James Freeman Clarke, and others does not seem to lack intellectual vigor; and the forty years that saw the enrichment or creation of the Boston Public Library, the Boston Museum of Fine Arts, the Worcester Art Museum, the Wadsworth Athenaeum, the Yale School of Fine Arts, the Boston Symphony, the Boston park system, Boston University, Boston College, Smith, Wellesley, Simmons, Clark University, and M.I.T. would seem to exhibit a common concern for high culture at least as vigorous as that of the Golden Day.

The unifying element is that set forth in Morison's charming *One Boy's Boston:* "Despite all the sneers and jeers at 'Proper Bostonians,' 'Boston Brahmins,' and the like, there was a remarkable pattern of living here that existed nowhere else in the United States. When a family had accumulated a certain fortune, instead of trying to build it up still further to become a Rockefeller or Carnegie or Huntington and then perhaps discharge its duty to society by some great foundation, it would step out of business or finance and try to accomplish something in literature, education, medical research, the arts, or public service." This seems to me to differ from the tensions of the fifties. The basis of this philosophy was obviously laid long before the Civil War, but the flowering of this attitude was in the era commonly described as the period of New England decline.

It may be well to particularize. In the first place, writers of the Golden Day did not all cease with the abolition of slavery. Bryant, gone to New York, it is true, was active for twenty-five years after Sumter. Whittier after 1860 published almost twenty volumes before his death in 1892, most of them repetitious but among them *Snow-Bound,* his masterpiece. Emerson produced nothing striking after 1860, but his fame and influence steadily grew. Longfellow published his great translation of Dante from 1865 to 1869, his *Tales of the Wayside Inn* (which includes the magnificent "Saga of King Olaf") from 1863 to 1873, wrote most of his finer lyrics between 1872 and 1882, and completed his vast religious trilogy,

Christus: A Mystery, in 1871. Holmes's *Breakfast-Table* series, begun in 1857, was not complete until 1891; his influential volume, *Medical Essays,* was published in 1883. Lowell's greatest service was possibly his diplomatic career between 1877 and 1885. Agitators and innovators had now become influential literary men or classics.

This transformation in repute and influence was brought about by a number of causes, among them an increased American interest in biography and a remarkable campaign of propaganda. Files of the *Publishers' Weekly* reveal the growing interest in biographical writing, given impetus by the centennial year of 1876, by curiosity concerning leaders in the Civil War, by a simultaneous increase of biographical writing in Great Britain, and by a feeling toward the end of the century that a great age was passing and needed to be memorialized. Books of reminiscence, autobiography, letters, and biography by or about these New Englanders form impressive clusters of titles in the years from 1880 to 1910. The effect was to emphasize unity, and as American literary history became standardized, the great New England writers became central.

New England also then produced its greatest literary propagandist since James T. Fields. This was Horace E. Scudder, born in Boston in 1838 and dying in Cambridge in 1902. In the late sixties he went to work for the future Houghton Mifflin Company, with whom he remained the rest of his active life. He founded the *Riverside Magazine for Young People,* rival of that other influential New England periodical, the *Youth's Companion.* He ran the Riverside Literature Series of texts for schools and colleges. The first number was by Longfellow, the second and third by Emerson, the fourth by Whittier, the fifth by Lowell, the sixth by James T. Fields. He helped create the original American Men of Letters series, for which he wrote a life of Lowell; and if it could not ignore Cooper, Poe, Simms, and Nathaniel Parker Willis, it went down the whole New England line. He got out superb collected editions of Hawthorne, Emerson, Longfellow, and the rest. He created the Cambridge Poets series, one-volume editions in which excellent scholarship was lavished on writers like Whittier and Holmes. He went about the country addressing teachers' meetings, urging that young America be exposed to the best that had been said in the United States; not unnaturally the best that had been said frequently turned out to be books published by his firm. He edited the *Atlantic* from 1890 to 1898. He made it impossible for any American schoolchild to be ignorant of the New England tradition.

I add parenthetically that the alleged Indian summer of New England was also the golden age of Boston printing and publishing, a period beside which the era of James T. Fields seems awkward and amateurish. I have in mind as examples not merely the fine scholarly work published by Ginn and Company and D. C. Heath but also the typographical excellence of John Wilson and Sons in Cambridge, printers of the collected works of Parkman, among other books; and in another sphere, the books brought out by Stone and Kimball in Cambridge and by Thomas B. Mosher in Portland, Maine, all influenced by the designs of William Morris and the decorative style of the "Art Nouveau" movement.

In support of the thesis that the New England mind lost energy after 1865, it is sometimes argued that reformers ran out of steam. This depends upon what one means by reform. If Emerson's "Divinity School Address" demands a reformed theology, Longfellow and Whittier continued to sap the foundations of orthodoxy long after the Civil War. The postbellum period was the flowering time of Phillips Brooks, James Freeman Clarke, George A. Gordon, and others in Christian theology, and of Solomon Schindler in shaping Reform Judaism. The Free Religious Association began in Boston; small in numbers, it was influential enough to color the World Congress of Religions held at the Columbian Exposition of 1893, and it patronized two magazines, the *Radical* and the *Index,* either of which had a circulation ten times that of the *Dial.* The *Index,* which ran from 1870 to 1886, one scholar describes as the "finest liberal religious journal in America." Octavius B. Frothingham, John Weiss, David A. Wasson, Francis Ellingwood Abbott, Felix Adler, Frank Lester Ward, and Cyrus A. Bartol, all connected with the Free Religious Association, are not names to be shrugged off.

Three great religious sects have been created in the United States: Mormonism, Spiritualism (in part), and Christian Science. The Boston area was so far important to Spiritualism that Spiritualist camp-meetings were once held at Walden Pond; and Christian Science is of course almost wholly a New England creation. In some sense Boston theological liberalism in the period goes back to transcendentalism, and all this can scarcely be dismissed as religious lassitude.

If the inquiry be transferred from theology to philosophy, one finds no symptoms of intellectual decay. Yale remained philosophically conservative for some years, and at Harvard Francis Bowen hung on until the mid-eighties, but William James, the true heir of Emerson, was appointed there in 1872, transferred to the department of philosophy in 1880, and became a central figure in the most brilliant philosophical constellation the country has ever known—George Herbert Palmer, the winning teacher, Josiah Royce, the philosopher of the Absolute, George Santayana, the philosopher of naturalism, and Hugo Münsterberg, the psychologist. At a little distance were Charles S. Peirce and Chauncey Wright, whom Norton called one of the few great thinkers of America. Meanwhile John Fiske was propagandizing the evolutionary philosophy of Herbert Spencer and applying it as well to American development.

If Emerson had insisted upon the centrality of individual development, these thinkers sought like him to escape from the trap of determinism by insisting upon the moral will. John Fiske was, no doubt, a popularizer, but for that very reason his utterances are representative. In 1885 he argued that theism is the legitimate and necessary outcome of modern scientific thought, saying that "the doctrine of evolution, by exhibiting the development of the highest spiritual human qualities as the goal toward which God's creation had from the outset been tending, replaces Man in his old position of headship in the universe. . . . Man [is] the terminal fact in that stupendous process of evolution. . . . The whole tendency of modern science is to impress upon us ever more forcibly the truth that the entire knowable universe is an immense unity, animated throughout all its parts by a single principle of life." This may be the scientific fallacy of vitalism, but it is also a child of the Emersonian Over-Soul.

If one passes to the greater men, one notes how Josiah Royce insists there is no mechanically assured progress but that in human life, as in the universe, a moral will perpetually struggles to overcome evil. Life, he argues, is valuable enough to be tragic. "The only harmony that can exist in the realm of the spirit," he wrote, "is the harmony that we possess when we thwart the present but more elemental impulse for the sake of the higher unity of experience; as when we rejoice in the endurance of the tragedies of life, because they show us the depth of life, or when we know that it is better to have loved and lost than never to have loved at all." William James profoundly distrusted any doctrine of a block universe, an inert system, and in *The Will to Believe* he insists that "our faculties of belief were not primarily given us to make orthodoxies and heresies withal; they were given us to live by." "It is only," he adds, "by risking our persons from one hour to another that we live at all. . . . If this life is not a real fight, in which something is eternally gained for the universe by success, it is no better than a game or private theatricals from which one may withdraw at will. But it *feels* like a real fight,—as if there were something really wild in the universe which we, with all our idealities and faithfulness, are needed to reform." In the preface to *Interpretations of Poetry and Religion* (1900) George Santayana declares that human life "is not merely animal and passionate. The best and keenest part of it consists in that very gift of creation and government which, together with all the transcendental functions of his own mind, man has significantly attributed to God as his highest ideal." In view of the vigor of these asseverations of the meaning of individualism and the moral will, all, as it were, following where the transcendentalists had pioneered, I for one am simply at a loss to understand the doctrine that intellectual vigor in New England somehow declined between the 1850's and the 1900's.

In the antebellum period efforts by those who had seen what higher education was in Germany and who wanted to modernize New England education failed; witness the frustrations of Ticknor, Everett, and Bancroft. In the postbellum period one traces the most extraordinary revolution American higher education has ever experienced. At Yale William Graham Sumner and at Brown President Elisha Andrews won hard-fought victories for the modern concept of academic freedom and responsibility. At Yale the creation of the School of Fine Arts in 1869 and at Harvard the appointment of Charles Eliot Norton in 1873 to teach the history of the fine arts virtually created a new discipline. In 1861 Yale conferred the first Ph.D. ever given in the United States. The opening of the Massachusetts Institute of Technology in 1865 marked the beginning of what competent specialists have called the leading technical institution of the world; it is interesting to note that M.I.T. started as a land-grant college under funds created by the Morrill Act of 1862, the invention of Senator Justin Smith Morrill of Vermont, who served in Congress so long he became known as the Nestor of the Senate.

But the great name is that of Charles W. Eliot, called to the presidency of Harvard in 1869, to become in all probability the most famous university president in American history. Educated as a scientist, he reshaped the whole range of higher education. He mediated between the traditional concept of the American college and the European concept of the university. Between 1869 and 1878 he transformed Harvard. He energized graduate work. He established there the principle that the professor is master in his own classroom. By bringing Langdell to the Law School, he created a totally new system of legal education. He abolished the lingering sectarianism of the Divinity School. He modernized the Medical School—nay, he may almost be said to have created it. John Fiske said of Eliot's epochal inaugural address: "I never before heard a speech as grand and impressive"—a comment surely as memorable as Holmes's much quoted remark that Emerson's "The American Scholar" was "our intellectual Declaration of Independence." As for the continuity of New England thinking, Eliot wrote in 1903: "When I had got at what proved to be my life work for education, I discovered in Emerson's poems and essays all the fundamental motives and principles of my own hourly struggle against educational routine and tradition, and against the prevailing notions of discipline for the young." Once again, where is the intellectual falling away?

I shall say nothing of the fine arts in this period, though the work of Richardson is surely as impressive as that of Bulfinch and a painter like Winslow Homer is the peer of a painter like Washington Allston. I cannot pause on the development of music in New England, though Gilbert Chase devotes a whole chapter in his *America's Music* to the Boston musical classicists. Admirable as the generations of the Sillimans, Gray, and Agassiz were, their work was at least equalled by that of later biologists, physicists, chemists, and geologists. It would take a long time to trace the enrichment of study and research in the humanities and the social sciences in the postbellum period.

I conclude by glancing all to briefly at the complex pattern of politics in the period. New England educated three or four presidents from outside the area—William Howard Taft at Yale, and the two Roosevelts—and later put two New Englanders into the White House. It sent influential men into the Cabinet; for example, James G. Blaine, and a variety of notable representatives to Congress, ranging from Ben Butler to Senator George Frisbie Hoar. It produced eminent jurists like the younger Holmes. The work of the second Charles Francis Adams, writer of *Chapters of Erie and Other Essays,* member of the state railroad commission, and later chairman of the board and president of the Union Pacific, requires no comment; it exhibits a tradition of civic and business responsibility.

Moreover, though it is often assumed that after the Emancipation Proclamation, antebellum zeal for change let down, one notes that most of the reformers who survived the war continued to be active, Sumner, Garrison, George William Curtis among them. Lowell, not usually thought of as a reformer, bitterly denounced the corruption of the Grant administrations, defined the United States as the land of broken promises, and wrote in a poem of 1872:

> . . . now that "Statesmanship" is just a way
> To dodge the primal curse and make it pay,
> Since office means a kind of patent drill
> To force an entrance into Nature's till,
> And peculation something rather less
> Risky than if you spell it with an *s*,
>
> . . . .
>
> With generous curve we draw the moral line;
> Our swindlers are permitted to resign.
>
> . . . .
>
> Steal but enough, the world is unsevere,—
> Tweed is a statesman, Fisk a financier.

In 1887 he turned Mugwump, declaring that Cleveland was "the best representative of the higher type of Americanism we have seen since Lincoln was snatched from us."

The most picturesque among the older men was, of course, Wendell Phillips, who, after the Civil War, thundered against drink, pled for woman suffrage, denounced the wrongs of Ireland, fought for the Negro, battled

against imported contract labor, opposed Biblical funda-
mentalism, plumped for public education, advocated labor's right to organize, and spoke up for the eight-hour
day. State Street merchants, who had cut him before the
Civil War, had taken to greeting him again—until he
proved an unreconstructed leftist. Here is a characteristic
passage from a speech of 1872 before the shoemakers'
union:

> Take a power like the Pennsylvania Central Railroad
> and the New York Central Railroad, and there is no
> legislative independence that can exist in its sight. As
> well expect a green vine to flourish in a dark cellar as
> to expect honesty to exist under the shadow of these
> upas-trees.

This did not altogether please the bankers. Reform,
moreover, did not stop with the death of Phillips in 1884.

Those who identify the New England mind from 1865
to 1915 with the genteel tradition have of course no
difficulty in dismissing whatever is not in the genteel
tradition as having nothing to do with the New England
mind. Three matters of national import should, however,
give us pause. The first is that Benjamin Orange Flower
migrated to Boston from Philadelphia in the eighties to
edit in succession the *American Spectator,* the *Arena,*
and, after an interval, the *Twentieth Century Magazine*
in 1909; and though he was virulently anti-Catholic and
inclined to psychical research, he made these periodicals,
particularly the *Arena,* national forums for discussing
liberal, progressive, and leftist ideas. The second is that
young liberals and radicals from the West—for example,
Hamlin Garland—flocked to Boston because Howells,
long editor of the *Atlantic* (his New England novels are
more searching than their pleasant style implies), the

Arena while it lasted, and organizations like the Free Religious Association and the Radical Club seemed to show that Boston was still the home of progressive thinking. The third is that when Edward Bellamy of Chicopee Falls published *Looking Backward,* at Boston in 1884, he validated this assumption, produced a book that sold a million copies, and laid the foundation of a chain of Nationalist Clubs that foreshadowed later progressive political ideas. But all this, and more, is analyzed in Arthur Mann's *Yankee Reformers in the Urban Age,* of 1954, and Geoffrey Blodgett's *The Gentle Reformers,* of 1966.

Valuable as the contributions of New England to national politics might be, and admirable as was the protection of liberal thought in the eighties in contrast to the harrying of the abolitionists in the forties and fifties, the weakness of the elite group was in political life. If they retained power in the professions, finance, publishing, the traditional colleges and preparatory schools, and of course the upper-class urban Protestant churches, they gradually lost their hold on local and state governments to representatives of the "New Americans." It was one thing to belong to the Dante Society, another thing to deal with local Italians, one thing to admire Catholic art abroad and another thing to talk with Catholic priests in Boston. Two cultures developed side by side, a Protestant one and a Catholic one, and though the relations between them were never as icy as those between the Protestant School Board and the Catholic School Board of Greater Montreal, there was a good deal of suspicion on each side. Moreover, a third, Jewish culture also developed, and in more recent years one is conscious of a fourth, a Negro one. It is, however, one thing to regret racial, religious, and social prejudices among these groups, prejudices that have too often operated to harm the cultural and political welfare of the commonwealth, and another thing to say that the New England mind, even within the limits of the Yankee and the Brahmin traditions, has somehow declined. I am bold enough to suggest that the conventional statement should be reversed and that the true flowering of New England comes after, not before, the Civil War. Its unity was greater and its influence was wider. It is no derogation of the generation that produced *Walden,* and *English Traits,* and *The Scarlet Letter,* and *Moby Dick,* to say that this was good planting. The proof of it is that the generation of Charles W. Eliot and Winslow Homer, Justin Winsor and William James, Arthur Twining Hadley and Henry Hobson Richardson, Willard Gibbs and Edward Bellamy have reaped the harvest that they sowed.

THE SCHOLAR AS AMERICAN

I wish to examine our theory and practice in carrying out two ideals of research common to science and scholarship. In the light of this discussion I shall then turn to American studies as a humanist sees them. The two ideals are contemplation and internationality. I begin with contemplation.

The theoretical aim of pursuing knowledge is contemplation in the Aristotelian sense. This truth is exemplified by the supposed intellectual superiority of pure over applied science. The pure scientist engages in fundamental research; that is, he makes inquiries which have for their ideal nothing short of understanding the structure of things, or, in the long run, contemplation. In one sense the doctrine never dies that the scientist thinks God's thoughts after Him, but in the absence of fideism from the modern laboratory let us say that the scientist uncov-

This address was delivered at Harvard University, October 3, 1960, to mark the inauguration of the new Abbott Lawrence Lowell Professorship of the Humanities, to which I had been elected. The address was printed in pamphlet form for private distribution, and portions of it appeared in the *Harvard Alumni Bulletin.*

ers a pure intellectual order, or even an unsullied and primal anarchy. If the God of revelation has been transformed into a *deus absconditus,* the scientist nevertheless continues to try to comprehend the basic *qualia,* the primary behavior of matter, whether its pattern be consonant with human reason or no. If science could miraculously reach its goal tomorrow, all that would be left for us to do would be to enjoy the majesty of anarchy, the majesty of order, or the majesty of God.

What is theoretically true of science seems to me also true of social science and the humanities. If we have not reduced the social sciences to universals, it is not for lack of trying. We think the nineteenth century naïf for cherishing a dream that general social principles could be simply stated, but I observe it is the sophisticated twentieth century that produces grandiose sweeps through time and society by Spengler, Pareto, H. G. Wells, Mannheim, Meinecke, and Toynbee, Mr. Toynbee ending with a revival meeting. In the humanities, though the search for universals is less evident, the humane ideal is Man. In subjects like aesthetics and modern criticism dogma abounds. The implication of much pseudo-philosophic interpretation is that the importance of writers like Melville, Kafka, and Sartre and of painters like Munch, Dali, and the German Expressionists lies in their sense of universal absurdity or of universal frustration, just as contemporary interpretation of writers such as Dickens, Dostoievsky, and Mark Twain underlines human imbecility. I do not applaud the doctrine, I merely point to it—a search for universals in succession to the belief of Winckelmann or Goethe that art is ideal form. Much in modern metaphysics seems to move in the same direction and says that the condition of humanity is a condition of being perpetually well deceived.

Expressions of admiration for the pursuit of knowledge as contemplation are ceremonially proper at the inauguration of university presidents, academic centennials, and the dedication of new buildings. In less exalted moments we realize that the goal of contemplation is realizable only in a university of archangels. One does not have to be an instrumentalist to know that in fact research is conditioned by more mundane considerations. If we took away from our laboratories the millions poured into them through government contracts involving national defence, a kind of scientific collapse would follow. If we then subtracted other millions that come from industry, and if industry should simultaneously close its research institutes and discharge its companies of industrial chemists, workers in biologicals, engineers, tenders of digital computers, personnel experts, and hired inventors, our graduate schools would shrink. Advances in medicine, moreover, commonly spring from specificity —man's irritation at his inability to cure a disease, his horror of suffering, his desire to solve the population problem, his dislike of growing old. In the field of mathematics one notes with amusement that the beginnings of the probability theories on which much modern calculation depends are found in gambling; and though Pascal's letters occasioned by de Méré's desire to win at games of chance are cited in support of the injunction: "Let the research man alone—you never can tell what he will turn up," the inquiry was mean in origin, just as the discoveries of Pasteur were occasioned by the profit motive of French vignerons. I do not deny the grandeur of the long-run results, nor am I saying that all research begins ignobly. I merely observe that research is commonly conditioned by more practical interests than contemplation. Possibly, indeed, the greatest effectual cause of research is that ignoblest of motives, the publish-or-perish theory alleged to be true of universities dedicated to pure intelligence.

Corollary to the contemplative theory is the theory that knowledge is, or ought to be, unconditionally international; and Soviet Russia is cited as a glaring instance of the perversion of this principle. Probably only astronomers, mathematicians, and musicologists work without reference to their native tongues, their native lands, and their native cultures, and even among them there are shocking falls from grace. At the other extreme the tensions apparently endemic in the teaching of modern languages are an odd commentary on unconditioned internationalism. Art historians, moreover, insist that schools of painting emerge from particular times, places, and cultures. Literary theorists, it is true, declare that Plato, Dante, Shakespeare, and the Bible are universal, but if you ask them why by their own logic the *Koran,* the *Panchatantra,* the poems of the Chinese *Shi-Kiang,* and the *Araucana* of Ercilla are not equally universal, they are forced back upon the divisive power of cultures: all masterpieces are equal, but some are more equal than others. In scientific history we note how often, whether the question concern pure knowledge (as in the quarrel between Newtonians and Leibnizians over fluxions) or applied science (witness international disputes as to who originated the steamboat), unconditioned internationalism has a hard time of it. I learned last year, for example, that the Russians invented the Land camera. Even philosophers and physicists do not live in the difficult air of the iced mountain topis, they are perforce Englishmen or Chinese, Jews or Christians, Europeans or Asians, communists or democrats, writers of French, Hebrew, German, Dutch, or Spanish in the first place, disembodied international intelligences only later and at a distance. Here again I am not being consciously cynical. The wonderful thing is not that the international ideal breaks down, the wonderful thing is that it exists. What I am saying is that we shall not attain it until the war drums throb no longer and the battle flags are furled in the parliament of man.

The flags have not been taken down, a fact that brings us face to face with the great existing discrepancy between theory and fact in the pursuit of knowledge. We take it as a matter of course that the prime allegiance of an American scientist or scholar is to flag, country, and culture, and only secondarily to the dispassionate pursuit of an international, or, if you like, a supra-national, pattern of truth. Great areas of the earth's surface—for example, mainland China—are closed to him by governmental fiat, and it is in vain that he protests that ignorance of China does no good either to the nation or to knowledge. Access to other areas—for example, countries with which the United States has no diplomatic relations or only frigid ones—is made difficult, though his motive be as pure as archaeology and as non-political as the search for a new plant. His relations with the intellectuals of other nations sometimes expand or contract with the international thermometer. At one period it is a kind of treason to correspond with members of the Russian Academy of Sciences, for example; at another our government hires an American scientist to go to Moscow and complains if he will not go. This kind of thing is not new —one thinks of the repudiation in 1789 by Catherine the Great of the French *philosophes*—but it is nevertheless a restriction upon internationalism.

More fundamental is the command laid upon intellectuals by government, explicit or implicit in the secrecy code governing research in projects allied to national defence. Not only must the scientist put his brains and his discoveries at the service of government in the first instance and of mankind afterwards, but the institutions that employ him submit to some measure of political control. The convulsive spurts by which research moves forward in certain areas—for instance, the exploration of space—are a function of this situation, less the product of pure reason than a mixture of curiosity, national pride, government contracts, and fear. If a Russian scientist defects to the free world, we, after due police investigation, hail him as a brand snatched from the burning; if a scientist defects from the free world to Russia, he becomes a Benedict Arnold of the intellect. The internationality of research has been so far colored that each side behaves like sports writers covering a football game; and the scientist, remote though his work may be from politics, is inevitably affected by the emotions engendered. How far we have drifted from the international ideal one can measure from the careers of a distinguished family of Swiss scientists whose combined lives ran from 1654 to 1782. Jacques Bernoulli traveled, taught, and published in Switzerland, France, England, and Holland; Jean taught in Holland, France, and Switzerland; Nicholas was a professor at Berne and at St. Petersburg; and Daniel held appointments at St. Petersburg and Basle and won ten separate prizes at Paris. Yet these are the years of the wars of Louis XIV, of Charles X, of Catherine the Great, of the War of the Austrian Succession and of the Seven Years War, besides innumerable lesser conflicts.

Social scientists are also involved in nationalism. We have no real party of the left in this republic and no left-wing economists or sociologists to speak of. The economic expert sent abroad is expected to expound free enterprise and make democracy work in undeveloped countries. As new nations arise we think of them as enlisting on our side only as they develop representative governments resembling our own or that of the British, even though the representation be formal only. Our economic missions tacitly assume that the backwardness of a foreign people has some mysterious connection with its lack of industrialization—one speculates about what we would have recommended to the Athens of Pericles—and that mind would be, indeed, daring which ventured to inquire into the philosophic difference between the propaganda of the Americans and the propaganda of the communist countries as theorists of happiness. Possibly there are no absolutes in the social sciences, but when we purged our universities of radical thought, we reduced social theory to what Kenneth Galbraith in *The Affluent Society* calls the conventional wisdom. His book concludes with this enigmatic metaphor: "To furnish a barren room is one thing. To continue to crowd in furniture until the foundation buckles is quite another." Conventional wisdom, he suggests, is still mostly engaged with furniture manufacturing, for such is our public policy, and the pressures of government upon many social scientists virtually forbid them to consider the affirmative values of any radically differing culture. To this rule-of-thumb generalization there is one exception: nowadays there is a certain nostalgic quality in the popularity of anthropology. Like Gauguin, some anthropologists hint that happiness and stability are not necessarily functions of affluence, but it is virtually un-American to say so.

My analysis has touched the humanities but incidentally. Humanistic scholarship has responded to modern American nationalism in two extreme fashions, one which turns away from nationalism, at least in theory, and one which accentuates it. The first is the movement of general education which abandons national lines, sets up lists of great books in translation, and creates courses of the type represented in our own catalogue. The second is represented by the manifold programs in American studies. The commitment of both programs is, I think, to the proposition that the United States is a great and powerful bastion of "freedom," protecting the culture of the West from a great Slavic threat across the Atlantic and from, a vast yellow peril across the Pacific. Both programs throw upon the scholar an enormous responsibility; and I now propose to inquire how in the American field this responsibility is being met.

It seems to me that a curious and important change of outlook has occurred. When at this university in 1837 Emerson examined scholarship and uttered what the elder Holmes characterized as our intellectual declaration of independence, he looked forward, not back. He declared he read with joy of the auspicious signs of the coming days. On the whole our programs in American studies do not read with joy the auspicious signs of the coming days, and, interpreting history, they translate the cultural pessimism of the present into historical ambiguity. A major mode of interpreting the American past presently assumes that the American dream is only a dream—that is, an illusion to be taken apart by contemporary scholars superior to illusion. The frontier in this interpretation was not a place for brave hearts but a refuge for the neurotic. The missionary movement of the nineteenth century was only formally an attempt to bring souls to Christ; viewed realistically, it was a mode of extending the export trade. The anger of abolitionist and muckraker was not righteous indignation at wrong, but fanaticism or naïveté. The spacious days of the founding fathers become the lost world of Thomas Jefferson. Of course I oversimplify; nevertheless our present mode of analyzing the national culture would profoundly puzzle Emerson and Whitman, Lincoln and Jefferson.

I read in the preamble of Jefferson's bill for education (1778): "It becomes expedient for promoting the publick happiness that those persons, whom nature hath endowed with genius and virtue, should be rendered by liberal education, worthy to receive, and able to guard the sacred deposit of the rights and liberties of their fellow citizens." I read in an address delivered in 1925 by Mr. Justice Cardozo to certain law school graduates: "You will study the wisdom of the past, for in a wilderness of conflicting counsels, a trail has there been blazed. You will study the life of mankind, for this is the life you must order, and, to order with wisdom, must know. You will study the precepts of justice, for these are the truths that through you shall come to their hour of triumph. Here is the high emprise, the fine endeavor, the splendid possibility of achievement, to which I summon you and bid you welcome." I suggest that these two utterances, a century and a half apart, have behind them a cultural dignity, a fusion of what is nationally desirable and what is internationally desirable. I suggest also that if we are in fact the last, best hope of Western man, if we have by force or circumstances become the principal guardian of a cultural tradition older than Homer, we in American studies must begin to inquire whether the parochialism and the pessimism now fashionable in the field can long continue. When I read in academic quarterlies that—I paraphrase—a sense of bewilderment and a refusal to come to terms with reality is the trademark of classic American literature, or that *The Adventures of Huckleberry Finn* is really a disguised version of Dante's Inferno, or that the reason William Faulkner does not write about normal people is that he doesn't think people are normal, I wonder what has happened to our sense of humor. I also wonder what has happened to the great tradition of Western humanism in relation to the problem of American life.

What is that problem? Let us return to the fountains. Let us ask ourselves what is the central issue before the humanist engaged in maturely interpreting the American scene.

Into the New World a rich and complex Old World culture—cultures would be the better word—was transplanted with extraordinary rapidity. The environment into which it came was unprecedented in the experience of Western man. The mountains were higher, the rivers were vaster, the climate more varied and violent, the natives stranger than anything he had ever known. Space and sky and forest were enormous. It was not Asia, it was something as queer, so to say, as landing on the moon.

This culture flowed from Europe westward in two great parallel streams. One of these, Latin, Catholic, and Mediterranean, spread over South America, Central America, Mexico, and most of the Caribbean, and at one time or another reached as far north on the one coast as the Carolinas, and on the other, San Francisco Bay. The organization of this culture, Spanish and Portuguese, was, as it were, *sui generis*. Its special characteristics affect us in the United States to this day. It retained its colonial status longer than did the culture of North America, but it was also in some ways and for that reason more mature. The place held by religion in it was radically different from the place held by religion in the future United States. During its spread in the New World it encountered three native cultures more sophisticated and advanced than anything north of the Rio Grande—the Aztec, the Mayan, and the Incan—and it absorbed and still exhibits many of the components of these cultures. Moreover, its attitude towards the native races, once the initial period of slaughter was over, differed basically from the traditional attitude of North America. Latin-American culture developed an economy, an educational system, and a set of social values not found in British North America. The Spanish and Portuguese languages carry with them their own psychology; and the difference between the *personalismo* of the Latin-American and the rugged individualism of the North American entrepreneur is more than a problem of translation and semantics, it is a problem of radical differences in outlook.

This culture of the South has been in constant active contact with the culture of the North in the New World from before the time English seadogs were singeing the king of Spain's beard down to the tension between the Cuba of Fidel Castro and the United States of President Eisenhower and his successors. These tensions and this contact are at once central to, and complications of, the problem of American studies as commonly pursued. Probably the relations between the two cultures have been oftener relations of hostility—witness the Mexican War—than of amiability, although periods that attempt understanding also develop—alas, more often in the political and economic spheres than in the cultural one.

American studies as usually pursued ignore this culture of the South. Americanists do not commonly read either Spanish or Portuguese, know little or nothing about Latin-American history, and are still more ignorant of its great cultural achievements like baroque architecture and of its rich and varied literature and its literary theory. Alfonso Reyes of Mexico, for example, was called at the time of his death by competent critics the last universal literary man, and fulfilled Archibald Macleish's demand for a return to the concept of the man of letters in the modern world.

Latin-American culture has been and is a dynamic element in the development of our own. It has, for example, furnished more than two thousand place names to the United States Postal Directory. Its languages have influenced American English as such simple examples as *rodeo* and *vamoose* immediately indicate. Its customs are part of our "westerns" on television. Its housing, its music, its dances, its scenery, its ruins, and its romance have been imitated and admired in the United States. One-third of the continental area of this republic was for a long period, as modern history goes, under the governance of Spanish viceroys or of Mexico. The largest single Christian church in the United States is identical with the dominant church in Latin America.

If we are the last, best hope of Western man, if we are to preserve and advance the institutions of Western Europe and of the Atlantic community, I suggest that the Latin-American approach to the problem of what it means to be this new man, this American, is of considerable philosophic importance to us. "American" values are not necessarily and uniquely those of North America. Alfonso Reyes' essay on what it means to be an American is, I think, superior in richness of thought and insight to most of the like North American essays on the same theme, from Crèvecoeur to Theodore Roosevelt. And I am, in fact, merely repeating Jefferson's urgent plea that one of the best ways to comprehend the culture of the New World is to study *all* the culture of the New World.

But it will be argued that for the humanist the problem of American studies primarily concerns the development of the United States. This history of North America, if we except the French-Canadians in Quebec, is the history of the transplantation into a New World mainly in the temperate zone of a culture predominantly Northern, Protestant, and Atlantic. We note at once in the famous cases of Jamestown, Plymouth, and Massachusetts Bay, that because of circumstances historically explicable, this culture began to adapt itself to its new environment and to develop new forms perhaps more quickly than did the culture of the South, though the point is debatable. Perhaps this exhibits the pragmatical spirit of the English tradition. Certainly differences between the Old World and the New seem to us, at least, earlier evident in the history of North America than in the history of Latin America. Shortly these differences become radical, particularly in politics, religion, and science, or rather the application of science to life. In the one area there develops the startling concept of a written constitution for a representative republic; in religion the concept of voluntary association; and in science the application of scientific principles to agriculture and industry, by and by on an enormous scale. In the North men turn against their ancestors, they denounce kings and aristocrats and the effete culture from which they sprang, they reduce religion to democratic principles, they seek to extirpate rather than to absorb races other than their own, or if not that, then to reduce them to perpetual servitude. Profound changes such as these go forward rapidly in the social and economic spheres whereas the arts remain cautious, conservative, and European. The praise of authors, painters, dramatists, sculptors, and architects here is long that they are no worse than Europe, sometimes as good, and occasionally better. We note how the recognition of Whitman comes late, and how we have to wait until the twentieth century for a Frank Lloyd Wright and how, after a thousand tries, we do not produce a dramatist of power until Eugene O'Neill.

All this is sufficiently complex, but the North American problem turns into something even more difficult than the adaptation of North European forms to a New World. In the closing decades of the last century and the opening quarter of this one the problem of adaptation and invention is immensely increased by the swarming hither of Slavs and Jews, Armenians and Greeks, and I am tempted to say Parthians and Medes and Elamites as well. They enrich our cultural life, but the problem of adaptation grows difficult, especially because their religions are not of the standard British types. Transplanted Europeans of the North—that is to say, the "Old Americans"—must revise their racial thinking, their religious acceptances, their theories of tolerance. They who struggled to liquidate the Indians and who enslaved the blacks scarcely finish an epic civil war with all its catastrophic consequences than they have to reinterpret their eighteenth-century principles. They have to equate with themselves and their traditions races and traditions hitherto remote and recondite in their experience. The problem is more than one of "Americanization," the problem is one of a transformation of culture. New and unexpected cultural forms appear, originating in quarters of the globe remote from Britain, Holland, Germany, France, and the Scandinavias—outlandish churches, odd ethnic groups, strange restaurants, new foods, inexplicable attitudes in law and politics, a babel of tongues that must be subdued into English, gaudy taste, new uses of Sunday, parochial schools, new burdens on public education, gangs organized on Sicilian lines, inherited contempt of group for group, new musical forms—these and a thousand other novelties affect everything from parades to public libraries.

For example, the traditional American school classics prove inadequate for this kaleidoscopic cultural pluralism, at once polyglot, industrial, and megalopolitan. Longfellow and Whittier will not do, the English Bible ceases to be a book in common, and it sometimes appears that only the *Julius Caesar* of Shakespeare and *Silas Marner* hold literature together in the schools. Highbrows, meanwhile, repelled by the vulgarity of mass entertainment, by a chain-store psychology, by an air-conditioned nightmare, remove Jonathan Edwards, Thoreau, Hawthorne, Melville, Henry James, and a few other writers to a special literary shrine. Yet none of these authors expresses America as the Declaration of Independence, a Fourth-of-July oration, Webster's "Reply to Hayne," and the Second Inaugural express America—that is, directly, plainly, and with simple affirmation.

A profound cleavage in the verbalization of American cultural values inevitably follows, something deeper than the difference among the academic intellectuals as a group, those who merely read good books, and those who principally devote themselves to television, the sports pages, and the picture magazines. The cleavage is, as it were, historical, not sociological only. On the one hand, as national interest in oratory dwindles and dies—and we underestimate, I fear, the importance of public discourse in American history—the function of Webster and Lincoln, Jefferson and even Will Rogers is taken over by programs of Americanization, loyalty oaths, and salutes to the flag by school children. On the other hand, the main stream of bellelettristic interest—that is, the force of literary criticism and of writing found satisfactory to that criticism—becomes like modern architecture a contribution to an international style—a style and an interpretation based on Freud, an Austrian; on Joyce, an Irishman; on French poets and critics congenial to T. S. Eliot, a British subject and to Ezra Pound, whose American connections are those of an expatriate. The point is not patriotism, the point is not a plea to return to oratory, the point is not to down-grade either literary theory or writers celebrated by that theory, the point is that literary studies as currently pursued have ceased to be that broad highway into a republican philosophy that was created by Irving, Bryant, Longfellow, Cooper, Simms, Lowell, Whittier, and Holmes in the nineteenth century. I must patiently repeat that this does not mean that Longfellow and Bryant were greater men, Melville and Hawthorne lesser ones. I am merely trying to describe a significant alteration in the usefulness of literature as now interpreted for the purposes of a truly humane, a truly scholarly interpretation of American culture. When one now asks, as Crèvecoeur asked in 1782, who is this new man, this American, the answer sometimes appears to be: he is a lonely soul lost in a wilderness of neo-Calvinism and midnight melancholy. This is an interesting answer but I am not persuaded it is a humane and scholarly one. To assume that the American writer is uniquely unhappy, to assume that American literature was grossly misunderstood until the appearance of D. H. Lawrence's *Studies in Classic American Literature* is to make an assumption possible only to those who mistake the *ipse dixit* of a highly subjective literary criticism for historical truth. Current identification of American literature with a message of darkness and revulsion—and nothing could have more horrified most of those who wrote it—is not cultural history.

It seems to me the humanist concerned for American studies and for a proper fusion of the national and the international orders of ideas must seek a higher level of discourse than this. He must begin by understanding that the United States is the first nation in history to be created on philosophic assumptions—assumptions that in fact boldly denied the premises of both Aristotle and Machiavelli. We came into being as a conscious culture exemplifying certain general ideas about the relation of the state to human life just as Soviet Russia came into being as a nation exemplifying general principles. Indeed, it is precisely because this is so that the great and dangerous tensions of the modern world exist. We did not invent these ideas, these principles, these assumptions, which some modern interpreters seem to join Rufus Choate in dismissing as mere glittering generalities. We got them from Europe, we got them from Western philosophy, from Western theology, from Western history, from the Western arts, from Western political theory, and we have become the chief proponent of the Western culture that shaped them and that, in our case, they have helped to shape. We therefore deal as scholars with a problem of such gravity, it may fairly be said that not failure but low aim is crime. Let us not fall into the error of Mr. Oliver Edwards in Boswell's *Johnson,* who said to the great lexicographer: "You are a philosopher, Dr. Johnson, I have tried, too, in my time to be a philosopher, but, I don't know how, cheerfulness was always breaking in." A solemn article in an academic journal assures me that cheerfulness will not break in, for I read there that humor has disappeared from letters for three stupendous reasons: comedy is intellectual, tragedy is a more natural form of expression, and no one, it seems, dares to handle the humorous incongruities of American life. I infer that the editors of this quarterly have never heard of James Thurber.

Such then is the antinomy of the age. Science, though its freedom is restricted by nationalism, works hopefully along an endless frontier. The humanists, though they are committed to a noble general view, when they turn to the national life, find small promise in either its philosophic assumptions or its artistic expressiveness, and even while we and the Russians try to project modern culture into outer space, deny to the culture thus to be colonized in other worlds any such qualities as reason, harmony, dignity, and joy. How, then, shall we strengthen our concept of Western man?

Well, there are at least three things not to do. The first is the method of uplift. From time to time there appear in newspapers and magazines editorials demanding that novelists abandon pessimism and write about the more smiling aspects of life, which are the more American. Serious writers very properly pay no attention to these exhortations. If we can imagine the Italian Optimists Club telling Dante he was driving business out of Florence by describing it as hell, we can also imagine Dante retorting that his concern was not with trade but with eternity. The world of the artist is not the world of Norman Vincent Peale.

Nor will we get anywhere by waving the American flag. We do not want to return to the charming trumpet-and-drum romances of the nineteen-hundreds in which villainous Tories were thwarted by a sound young patriot aided by a pure, sweet girl while General Washington looked on. The American Legion is an even worse judge of art than is the State Department; and the last thing that will help us is official art. Better anarchy than art or scholarship in which all the issues are predetermined.

There is still truth in Nietzsche's famous dictum that you must have chaos within you if you wish to give birth to a dancing star.

Nor, in the third place, is it a defence of the pessimists that they mean well. Misunderstanding Hardy's famous statement that to arrive at the best demands a look at the worst, those who stress the wickedness of man, the debility of society, the vacuity of culture, and the propriety of violence, degeneracy, and failure as themes for art argue, to be sure, that the profound sympathy they wish to evoke for the human predicament is on the side of the angels. It is. But this is to substitute emotionalism for philosophy. It may, indeed, be true that, contemplating Popeye, Lolita, Studs Lonigan, and that interesting character in Kafka who turns into an insect, I may be led to exclaim: "There, but for the grace of God, go I." But the grace of God is an understandable concept accepted as part of a coherent theology intellectually prior to the expression of pity by the great Methodist who first uttered this famous phrase. Man's inhumanity to man has made countless thousands mourn ever since Achilles mistreated the body of Hector, but to stop with this commonplace is to beg the central issue. Let us not mistake compassion, which is part of wisdom, for the whole of wisdom, which is the goal, at least, of the humanities.

What, then, is to be done? We cannot avoid nationalism if we would; we must understand Western Europe and the Atlantic Community if we are to defend it. The professional career and the educational philosophy of the distinguished president of Harvard whose name is given to the chair I occupy are in this context relevant. Member of an American family whose connections with this institution date from the early eighteenth century, Mr. Lowell, no less an American for doing so, interested himself in the political culture of Europe, and his famous work, *The Government of England,* published in 1908, is possibly the most distinguished interpretation of a foreign government and its processes ever written by an American scholar. In his inaugural address as president he struck out against the fallacy, current then as now, that the way to advance the American mind is to invent shorter and cheaper degrees. He said of the college that it ought "to produce, not defective specialists, but men intellectually well rounded, of wide sympathies and unfettered judgment . . . trained to hard and accurate thought." "One object of a university," he wrote, "is to counteract rather than copy the defects of the civilization of the day." To the end that superior minds might ripen into maturer scholarship he created the Society of Fellows, the record of which, recently published by Crane Brinton, is an endorsement of depth and enlargement of mind, not of a quickie degree. Mr. Lowell, says the historian of Harvard College, was impatient of intellectual mediocrities, C men, plodding graduate students, and faculty members who were merely useful. The revolution in college education begun under Mr. Lowell and happily continued by his successors has done much to diminish the proportion of C men in the college. So far as graduate work in the humanities is concerned, whether nationally or here, I am frank to say we could do with fewer mediocre minds and a less routine attitude towards the doctoral program. President Lowell declared that "the most vital measure for saving the college is not to shorten its duration, but to ensure that it shall be worth saving." I believe this statement to be true today of graduate work in the humanities, notably in the field of American studies.

Like it or not, we cannot avoid Europe nor continue to ignore that sister child of the Old World, Latin America.

Young Americanists simply do not know the European culture from which we spring. What passes for a command of foreign languages in our graduate schools has long been a scandal, one that perhaps the scientists, with their inventions of abstracts, can endure, but that the humanities cannot, for the obvious reason that you cannot abstract the great monuments of European thought and art. It is not in the languages only, it is likewise in general culture that we fail. If perchance the young Americanist knows a little European literature, he does not usually also know the arts, architecture, music, and philosophy, he does not understand that romanticism in Europe was a system of thought, not an eccentric cult, that monarchy was a living principle like communism, that the doctrine of the divinity of the people in Walt Whitman parallels and echoes the populist theology, so to speak, of Michelet, George Sand, Heine, and Manzoni. Moreover, the interests of these young scholars too often begin and end with fragments of the nineteenth and twentieth centuries, so that, despite the immense industry of scholars like Murdock and Miller, humanists in the American field do not understand the necessity of commanding the rich and varied literature of the periods of exploration and discovery, colonial and provincial creativity, and the weight and onset of the eighteenth-century debate over the relation between politics and aspiration, out of which the nation rose. In the single field of American education—and upon an enlightened electorate the founding fathers hoped to establish both a culture and a nation—matters have been so feebly pursued that only a few years ago the American Historical Association appointed a committee to urge that research be done. But is there anything more central than the educational pattern by which a culture is immortalized?

It will be said that these are impossible demands. But the university world has succeeded in adjusting itself to the impossible demand upon the human brain of modern astronomy, modern physics, modern mathematics. Comparative literature makes impossible demands. So does a proper degree in history. The study of American culture is, I suggest, one of the most difficult and demanding disciplines in the world of scholarship, but we cannot blink its difficulties. It is not a discipline for the C mind, and I think it important not to sophisticate the problem by easy and shallow solutions. This I believe not merely because the scholar cannot think otherwise, but also because the fate of the world may depend upon the ability of Americans to understand and express the origins, direction, and implications of American life. This is why I speak of the scholar as American. This is why, beneath the frustration fashionable as a theme in current fiction, beneath the noisy vulgarities of our supersonic age, beneath the anxieties and the bewilderment, I still believe it possible for the humanist, concerned about American values, to say with Judge Cardozo: "You will study the wisdom of the past, for in a wilderness of conflicting counsels, a trail has there been blazed. You will study the life of mankind, for this is the life you must order and, to order with wisdom, must know. You will study the precepts of justice, for these are the truths that through you shall come to their hour of triumph. Here is the high emprise, the fine endeavor, the splendid possibility of achievement, to which I summon you and bid you welcome."

EPILOGUE:
THE SHRINE
OF THE
WORD

THE SHRINE OF THE WORD

ENTHUSIASTS for communication theory, information retrieval, the digital computer as a labor-saving device, and, in some dimmer sense, structural linguistics, strive to reduce language to the stark simplicity of a shorthand system. Language can be treated mathematically, they think, in some black-and-white, either-or system in which or by which meaning cannot be mistaken. How many times does such and such a writer mention baseball in a treatise on social ethics? How often does the image of foam as the flower of the sea appear in Swinburne? Does the recurrence of "It is me" outnumber the recurrence of "It is I"? In such communication systems, which assume as a matter of course that formal grammatical terms have been ignorantly applied to language from without instead of developing through language from within, the only nuances possible resemble logarithmic

During his lifetime Robert Frost was accustomed to send out as Christmas greetings single poems of his, exquisitely printed by Joseph Blumenthal of The Spiral Press. Desiring to continue this custom after Mr. Frost's death, Mr. Blumenthal has solicited short essays from others in defense of printing and of literature. "The Shrine of the Word" was written for this purpose and distributed in December, 1967.

theory, repeating decimals, or any similar device borrowed from mathematics. "Communication" becomes quantitative, not qualitative, and the only difference between the style of Henry James and the style of a sports reporter, when you feed each into a machine, is that the number of countings possible in James is greater than that in the style of the reporter because James employs more words though the reporter has a more professional vocabulary.

There is much to be said for communication theory and for the computerizing of some sorts of verbal discourse. At the great Countway Library of Medicine in Boston, for example, a surgeon desiring to read up on some rarer form of kidney ailment to discover how other surgeons have treated it and what the chances of success may be, in place of turning over the indexes of innumerable medical journals, can through an information retrieval system recover all relevant cases from the literature of medicine in an astonishingly short time. He will, of course, have only the vaguest sense of the personality of the patient, the doctor, or the surgical nurse in charge, just as he will have little or no information about the actual operating room or the little human drama enacted within it or centering upon it—that compound of fear and hope, religious emotion and professional courage, bright-eyed interest or weariness that is part of the drama of any major operation. From the point of view of the profession, however, these are not the problem. The question is the best mode of treatment, and although the case history of the patient may be an important element in the several cases, everything else is minor or irrelevant. All operating rooms are more or less alike, all operations have in them some element of risk, all scientific procedure is, even at the highest level, a game of chance played against the unknown. What the surgeon wants is the Fact; that is, he wants verbal information as scrubbed, clean, objective, and antiseptic as the operating room.

In the Jefferson Medical College in Philadelphia hangs one of the great pictures in American art. This is "The Gross Clinic" by Thomas Eakins. In medical terms the picture is totally obsolete. The operating room is primitive beyond belief, or, more exactly, no one operates nowadays in an auditorium. None of the doctors surrounding the patient, whose livid thigh is the concentration point of the picture, has on a surgeon's gown, none of them wears surgical gloves, and they are all dressed as if for a wedding. The central figure, Dr. Gross, with his pince-nez in his right hand, is sombrely clad as a preacher or a statesman. He has apparently not followed the simplest principle of antisepsis. A figure under his right arm (a relative? a spectator? a student?) is, either through weariness or shock, shielding his face from the operation with the back of his hand, his fingers rigid and separated. Dimly seen in the background—indeed, *as* the background—the students, seated in rising tiers that descend to the low balustrade separating the floor from seats, can scarcely see what is going on, though it is evident that Dr. Gross is holding their attention. The source of the light is concealed, and the lighting is virtually theatrical: it illumines Dr. Gross's head, the patient's thigh, parts of the heads of the four men surrounding the patient, and part of the balustrade of the auditorium. For medical instruction the painting could be used as a perfect example of the old, bad ways of surgery.

Yet this great canvas tells us more about the dedicated spirit of a great physician than do all the cases retrievable by any information system. Dr. Gross's head is noble, the man is earnest, his face is a palimpsest on which the spectacle of human suffering and the struggle of science to alleviate it have written their history. His commitment both to the unconscious patient and to the students around him is absolute. The assistants are grave, alert, involved; the students, one of whom is caught in the light on the balustrade recording all he can in a note-book, are attentive. What one thinks of when one first sees the painting is not that the science is obsolete but that the problem of science and suffering is forever new, forever old. We know that Eakins toiled to get his medical details right. We cannot question the scientific exact-ness to the period of what he portrayed. Eakins was a realist who in the search for pictorial truth violated all the aesthetic canons of the decade. His picture is not pretty. Its realism so shocked contemporaries that he and it were labelled "brutal," and his great canvas was, so to speak, imprisoned in the hallway of a medical school rather than being exhibited on the wall of some great museum, where it belongs.

I can think off-hand of no literary treatment of the teaching of medicine comparable to Eakins' picture. But if I may be allowed a bit of sleight-of-hand work, let me say that the information retrieval system beautifully oper-ating in the Countway Library, an immense advance as a tool for procuring reliable information quickly, repre-sents the universe of Fact; and that Eakins' picture repre-sents another universe—the universe of the interpretative imagination that never scorns reality but looks beyond it to some greater truth. It is a product of Poetry in the largest, Greek sense of making or creating. Let us say that if we could translate the picture into literature, it would represent the Word.

The first verse of the Gospel of St. John runs: "In the beginning was the Word, and the Word was with God, and the Word was God." In the following verses, which deal mystically with the idea of creation as power, the creative process is sometimes called the Word and sometimes called the Light. The surgeon, faced with a special problem of a diseased kidney and how to treat it, rightly wants the Fact; Eakins, trying to show us the dignity and the responsibility of a great medical teacher, passes beyond the Fact to the Word. No conceivable information retrieval system can give us the Word in this sense; it can only assume as its premise that medicine operates within a universe of discourse of its own. A retrieval system may assume the dignity of learning and of teaching but it can only assume it, it cannot analyze it, or count it, or measure the difference between Eakins' picture and other pictures of medical men at work.

In the beginning was the Word. Most persons agree, I think, that the two men of the nineteenth century who came closest to being universal geniuses were Alexander von Humboldt and Johann Wolfgang von Goethe. When the first tried to record his total interpretation of the universe he drew upon both science and art and wrote his magnificent *summa,* the *Kosmos,* a work insufficiently known. The other, desiring to record both the aspirations and the limitations of learning, and desiring also to record the restless spirit of man with all the good and evil that restlessness brings upon the modern world, wrote *Faust.* One of the key scenes in the First Part of *Faust* is laid in Faust's study. Faust feels in him that quality of spiritual dryness the medieval theologians called *acedia,* something neither a walk in the green fields nor the applause of his fellow townsmen has done anything to cure. In a search for health he opens the New Testament to the Gospel according to John and reads: "In the beginning was the Word." He stops. He must translate it into

233

something else—shall I say like the structural linguists? He tries: "In the beginning was the Thought," but this won't do—thought is itself, in his sense, uncreative. He amends this to: "In the beginning was the Power" (*die Kraft*), but this is tautological. Finally he comes to: "In the beginning was the Deed"—a truly American assumption, though the play is theoretically laid in medieval Germany. Then, after a deal of circumambient hocus-pocus, Mephistopheles takes bodily shape before him. Faust has tried to replace the Word by the Fact ("Deed"), and in so doing he summons up the spirit that eternally denies. To substitute machinery for language is to deny.

Any set of like animals can communicate, and we amuse ourselves by tracking down the communication systems of dolphins, and bees, and ducks, and others. Only man is gifted with the Word. Translated into the mystery of pigment, the Word produces "The Gross Clinic." Kept in literary bounds, the Word produces *Kosmos* and *Faust*. Statistics do not move mankind.

It was undoubtedly a brilliant piece of empirical insight fortified by statistical observation to discover that the radius vector of the planets sweep over equal areas in equal time. Nobody, however, has gone to the barricades to attack or defend this proposition. The concept of the square root of minus one is a wonderful and ingenious invention: it lacks the emotional impact of these words: "All men are created equal," even though you cannot prove that they are and even though you can prove that the square root of minus one, given the premises of certain mathematical systems, has definite meaning. The pursuit of the intricate nothings out of which the atom is theoretically made up is a hunt more dazzling than anything the Greeks imagined about Artemis, and seems to be moving in the direction of a queer non-existence of matter in the usual sense in our universe. Put it along side of this passage from *The Tempest,* however, and the atom-smasher recedes in moral importance:

> . . . . like the baseless fabric of this vision,
> The cloud-capp'd towers, the gorgeous palaces,
> The solemn temples, the great globe itself,
> Yea, all which it inherit shall dissolve;
> And, like this insubstantial pageant faded,
> Leave not a wrack behind. We are such stuff
> As dreams are made on, and our little life
> Is rounded with a sleep.

You cannot put this vision into any conceivable information retrieval system, though you can put the individual words that make it up into such a system. But you will end only with lists of words.

The shrine of the Word is the Book. Some persons are, as I think rather prematurely, ushering the Book into oblivion. They seem unable to distinguish a volume containing the plays of Shakespeare from a volume containing the telephone directory. The Bible and the directory are both books, and the aim is swiftly to replace these obsolete objects in space, gawky as sections of two-by-fours, with tapes, or punch cards, or something else mechanical. These people get their ideas from theorists who talk about language as if language never develops beyond a stimulus-and-response mechanism. They talk about words and know nothing about the Word. You cannot treat Job so. Language, even the so-called "primitive" languages (the complexities of which should give us ample warning not to reduce them to stimulus-and-response only), are instruments for nobility of discourse about the gods, about ghosts, about life, about death, about tradition. Words, wrote Emerson in that little azure-colored book of his called *Nature,* as Carlyle dubbed it, are the signs of natural facts, but they go beyond facts, which Emerson dismisses somewhat unfairly as mere "pepper-corn informations." They go beyond facts to a panorama of history, of philosophy, of theology, of nature itself. He dares to claim that the axioms of physics translate the laws of ethics; and though we must of course gloss his physics as that of the Newtonian universe, change in physical theory does not carry with it an up-side-down revolution of the doctrine of the Word. Emerson cites several propositions from science that have, he says, a more extensive and universal sense when applied to human life; yet though we may question his physics, science remains perpetually unstable, whereas art is less so. "The Gross Clinic" is a faithful replica of a technical performance in the seventies of the last century, but it is not a line-drawing for an anatomy textbook. It passes beyond simple "reality" to the universal meaning of the worth and gravity and terror of the healing arts.

The shrine of the Word has been, and always must be the Book—that is, some physical container, whether it be an Assyrian brick or a modern paper-back, which comes into being for a single and unique purpose, one more miraculous than any information retrieval system. This purpose is to multiply indefinitely exact copies of a thought, or, if you prefer, thoughts, or more exactly the phenomenal appearance of the Word. The book, it is true, may wear out or vanish; when it does so in any important case we lament the loss, a lament that is in itself our tribute to language. Within the Word, because created by it, are Helen, Ulysses, Mr. Pickwick, George Washington, Abraham Lincoln, Iago, Hitler, Cinderella, Mahomet, Christ. These cannot be subsumed or analyzed or disposed of by any conceivable digital computer. One might as well try to take the latitude of the Seven Dwarfs and tabulate the gross annual income of Santa Claus. It is as impossible to reduce Gibbon's vision of eternal Rome decaying into a communication system as it is to hope that a group of chimpanzees playing with typewriters will produce a second "Lycidas."

The mechanization of "communication" is immensely useful, though immensely troublesome, but it is not useful in the greatest way of all, the way of the Word, that outward and visible form of the inward and spiritual grace we call literature, philosophy, religion, history, politics. The Word perpetually seeks permanence, and when the Word seems to us more than mere communication, we give it such permanence as mere mortality can create: we put it into a book. To suppose that the book is a transient phenomenon like a stone axe is to mistake communication for reality. Let us pay our bills and make our telephone calls by number systems, but let us also remember that the art of the Word and the art of the Book are two faces of the same enduring coin

HOWARD MUMFORD JONES

Howard Mumford Jones, who is now Abbott Lawrence Lowell Professor of Humanities, *Emeritus,* at Harvard University, was born in Saginaw, Michigan, and was educated at the University of Wisconsin and the University of Chicago. He has been a student, a teacher, a humanist, and a writer all his life.

He has held important professorships at the University of Texas, the University of North Carolina, and the University of Michigan, as well as at Harvard; and has served as Visiting Professor or occasional lecturer at numerous other institutions including M.I.T., the Hebrew University of Jerusalem, and most recently Middlebury College. Harvard, Tulane, Ohio State, Wisconsin, Northwestern, and other outstanding universities have awarded him honorary doctorates. He was president of the American Academy of Arts and Sciences, 1944–1951, and chairman of the American Council of Learned Societies, 1955–1959; his memberships in other scholarly societies are far too numerous to mention. He has written more than thirty books and has edited another dozen. His *O Strange New World* won a Pulitzer Prize in 1964.

When Mr. Jones has time off from teaching, lecturing and delivering commencement addresses, he does his writing in Widener Library and lives happily on Francis Avenue in Cambridge, Massachusetts.